(Re)Imagining Inclusion for Children of Color with Disabilities

SOYOUNG PARK

Harvard Education Press
Cambridge, Massachusetts

Paperback ISBN 9781682539583

Library of Congress Cataloging-in-Publication Data is on file.

Published by Harvard Education Press,
an imprint of the Harvard Education Publishing Group

Harvard Education Press
8 Story Street
Cambridge, MA 02138

Cover Design: Endpaper Studio

The typefaces in this book are Carrara and Gotham.

For Minyoung

May you never let the world tell you, "You can't . . . "

You already are.

CONTENTS

CONTENTS

Introduction

WHEN I WALKED INTO the room, a row of children stood lined up against the front wall of their second grade classroom. Others sat on the rug in front of them or stood to the side. All of the children held scripts in their hands. The class was preparing for a play they were going to perform for the entire school in just a few weeks. When the scene being practiced was finished, the children made moves to rearrange the classroom furniture for the next scene. One child, Javier, who has an individualized education program (IEP) for Other Health Impairment (ADHD), began pulling out chairs and climbing over tables. "Javier!" his teacher exclaimed. She placed her hands on her head, looked at me, and said, "Like a bull in a china shop."

Javier continued to rearrange the furniture in his way and then eventually sat down on a chair at the front of the room to take on his role as Second Narrator. Throughout the rehearsal, Javier flipped through the pages of his script, seemingly unsure of where the group was. His teacher told him repeatedly to focus on the highlighted lines, but he continued to flip the pages, frequently turning to the First Narrator seated beside him and asking, "What page are we on?" in a loud voice. His peer would look at Javier wide-eyed and would show him her own script to try and guide him. Both she and the classroom teacher cued Javier each time he had a line to read.

> At the end of the rehearsal, the children moved the classroom furniture once more to put everything back in its original place. While the children's desks were mostly positioned in clusters of four or five, Javier sat at a desk that stood on its own, like an island floating in the middle of the classroom. Perhaps sensing some surprise in my gaze, Javier's teacher turned to me and said, "I needed to put him on his own. I was worried about how he would feel, being isolated in this way. But he's actually assimilated to it quite well. And it's been a relief for the rest of the class."

The racialized segregation, isolation, and exclusion of children of color with disabilities in US schools often begins with a story like Javier's (all names of children, adults, and schools are pseudonyms). When I was collecting data at Javier's school, he was a second grader in a Spanish-English dual immersion classroom. His family had emigrated to the US from Mexico a few years before Javier was born. Javier received an attention deficit hyperactivity disorder (ADHD) diagnosis at the beginning of the year in second grade. His disability, coupled with his status as an English learner, seemed to justify his increased exclusion from his general education classroom and his peers, as he was regarded as a child in need of remediation across multiple realms. Javier's exclusion began long before his isolated seating arrangement described in the excerpt that starts this chapter. From frequently being pulled out of the classroom for English-language classes and special education services to regularly being sent to the principal's office or his former first grade classroom as disciplinary measures, Javier's time spent with his homeroom peers was limited to a couple of hours each day.

When he was in the classroom, Javier was set apart in a variety of ways. He was given different tasks than the rest of his peers, and he was often reprimanded for his behavior. At times, he was also asked to go to a separate part of the room and sit quietly due to actions that were deemed disruptive. This adult-guided isolation eventually translated to

Javier's peers' interactions with him as well. The other children in the classroom often scolded Javier, telling him to "stop" or "go away." When he tried to enter social interactions, he was frequently met with silence or refusal. Javier was the last child selected for group work or activities, and his efforts to contribute to collaborative tasks were ignored. Perhaps unsurprisingly, these exclusionary circumstances led Javier to further enact behaviors that others saw as troubling—speaking out of turn, getting up and moving around the room when the class was directed to sit, climbing on furniture, and turning classroom items into toys to play with. Javier was trapped in a vicious cycle, where his exclusion sparked behavior that led to further exclusion. What Javier did not experience was any effort to adapt the learning environment to better fit his learning style and interests. His ADHD and English learner status were regarded as hindrances to his learning—qualities that needed to be isolated and controlled, rather than as opportunities for more creative instructional practices that would foster genuine belonging for Javier.

Javier's story is unfortunately neither unique nor new. Children with disabilities have experienced segregation and isolation in schools since long before special education as a field was legally established.[1] Exclusionary practices are particularly prevalent among children of color with disabilities who, along with their families, perpetually face barriers to accessing high-quality, inclusive education.[2] In US schools, disproportionate segregation of children of color with disabilities begins in early childhood. Children of color with disabilities ages three to five are much more likely to receive their educational programming in separate classrooms or schools than are white children with disabilities of the same age. Along similar lines, children of color with disabilities ages six to twenty-one are significantly more likely to spend less than 40 percent of their school day in general education compared to their white counterparts. In an extreme form of exclusion, Black youth with disabilities are three times more likely to receive their educational services in a correctional facility than are white youth with disabilities.[3]

Even when children of color with disabilities do spend a majority of their school day in general education classrooms with their nondisabled peers, disciplinary practices are used as a means to disproportionately isolate them. Black children with disabilities are about 2.8 times more likely than their peers of other races to experience exclusionary discipline such as out-of-school suspensions or expulsions, and there is growing concern about the widespread use of exclusionary discipline for all students with disabilities who identify as Black, Indigenous, and people of color.[4] These patterns are prevalent even in the early childhood years. In 2021, 75 percent of children with disabilities ages three to five across all races experienced some form of suspension or expulsion compared to children without disabilities in the same age range. Black children with disabilities ages three to five were four times more likely than their white peers to experience out-of-school suspensions or expulsions lasting more than ten days.[5]

Segregation through service provision or disciplinary practices has been found to have negative consequences for children of color with disabilities. They receive minimal, if any, opportunity to interact with their nondisabled peers, are limited in their access to grade-level curricula and thus report feeling unchallenged and bored in school, demonstrate higher levels of absenteeism than their disabled peers who are more integrated into general education, are more likely to experience retention or to drop out of school, and are less likely to receive postsecondary education. All these outcomes have long-term impacts on the livelihoods of children of color with disabilities well beyond their years in school.[6]

The pushing-out of children of color with disabilities in schools is a critical problem that stems from and perpetuates systemic inequity at the intersection of race and disability. As Annamma, Connor, and Ferri (2013) argue, while segregation based on race would be illegal, segregation based on disability is permitted because it is seen as a "real" difference rather than a "socially constructed" one.[7] Special education is thus a vehicle for continuing to separate and oppress children of color in a post–*Brown v.*

Board of Education era.[8] In 1968, Dunn published what he called his "swan song," strongly critiquing his own field for maintaining race-based segregation (often tied to linguistic and class-based segregation) through the expansion of specialized classes. Dunn questioned whether specialized classes were truly necessary for the majority of children placed in them. He felt that general educators viewed segregated special education settings as a way to rid themselves of children they had difficulty teaching. Dunn observed that 60 to 80 percent of the children in specialized classes or schools were "from low status backgrounds": children of color, children from households that spoke languages other than English, and children from lower-class communities.[9] From his perspective, most of these children would benefit from structural and pedagogical changes in the general education setting so their learning needs could be met better—they would *not* benefit from further segregation and isolation.

Researchers and policy makers have examined this problem of segregation and exclusionary discipline among children of color with disabilities since Dunn published his seminal piece, and yet these injustices persist.[10] Underlying the systemic isolation of children of color with disabilities in special education is a deep-seated culture of schooling that is rooted in sociopolitical, historical racism and ableism.[11] These systems of oppression do not begin with segregated experiences, but rather start from the moment that a child of color is considered for special education eligibility. Racial disproportionality is an indicator of potential inappropriate identification for special education among children of color, which Dunn warned against in the 1960s. National data suggest that Black, Indigenous, and Latinx children are often overrepresented in special education.[12] Although Asian children are found to be underrepresented in special education, some research indicates that Asian children who are deemed eligible for special education may still undergo flawed identification processes that raise questions as to whether their eligibility is warranted.[13]

There are many possible explanations in the literature for why children of color might be erroneously referred to special education services, such as educator bias and deficit perspectives about children of color and their communities; lack of training on educational practices that are best suited for the range of linguistic and cultural diversity in a classroom, which negatively affects children's academic performance; and culturally biased and invalid assessment tools and identification processes.[14] Artiles and colleagues (2010) warn that individuals should not be faulted for factors such as bias and lack of training. Rather, the underlying problem exists in the cultural norms of schooling. In other words, schooling in the US has been structurally designed to perpetuate oppressive systems and processes that contribute to inappropriate identification.

WHAT ARE THE CULTURAL NORMS OF SCHOOLING IN THE US?

Growing up in the suburbs of New York City as an Asian American child in a Korean immigrant family, I was aware of the cultural norms of schooling from a very young age. The district that I was a part of was majority Black, followed by white and Latinx as the second- and third-largest racial groups. From kindergarten through eighth grade (after which I left the school district), I was one of three or four Asian children in my entire grade. In my first week of kindergarten, I was pulled out of the classroom to attend English as a Second Language classes, which I did until the teacher realized that I spoke English fluently. Throughout elementary and middle school, I experienced academic tracking, which divided students along racial lines. My classes were majority white, with a sprinkling of Black students, Latinx students, and Asian students. Our teachers were considered the best, our academic content the most challenging, and our peer group the most advanced.

In my schooling, there were strict expectations around behavior, to which we had to adhere to avoid punishment: only speak when spoken to, sit still and tall, walk in straight lines, respond in full sentences using "proper" grammar, and do your work independently and silently. All free talk and laughter were to be reserved for snack, lunch, and recess. Learning was equated with listening to your teacher, writing down what they wrote on the board, and answering questions (which often had a right or wrong answer) when called upon. My classes were characterized as "good" because of how quiet and presumably focused we were, whereas the other classes in the school were seen as loud and rowdy, and therefore "bad." While I was often praised for demonstrating respectful behavior and strong academic performance, I felt othered by the white, Eurocentric curriculum; offensive questions from peers and adults about my food, language, facial features, and family; and my inability to show my full self, which included a silly, imaginative, and sometimes loud side, which was reserved for home. I distinctly remember thinking, "I have to be the whitest, most buttoned-up version of myself to belong here."

I know that my experience is not unique. There are many others, of all races, genders, socioeconomic statuses, abilities, and nationalities, whose stories are similar to my own. I also know from my years as a classroom teacher, teacher educator, and educational researcher that the culture of schooling that I experienced as a child has not changed as much as I would hope, particularly for children of color, children with disabilities, children from lower socioeconomic backgrounds, children labeled "English learners," and children who sit at the intersections of these various identities. Adair and Colegrove (2021) explain that schooling for our youngest learners of color has become increasingly rigid over time. While white children are "offer[ed] schooling that is engaged, dynamic, and sophisticated," children of color are offered "rigid and narrow schooling that is fixated on compliance." They also caution, "This *segregation by experience* results in short- and long-term injustices that perpetuate an intentional, racist denial of access and opportunity."[15] They go on to explain:

> Most young children in the United States today have narrower and more rigid learning experiences at school than children did twenty

> years ago (Bassok, Latham, and Rorem 2016). Children are having to sit still for longer and longer periods, completing tasks they do not choose in positions and spaces they do not control. . . . This loss has disproportionately impacted young children of color because teachers, schools, and districts serving children of color have to navigate pressures to be efficient, keeping content aligned with what will be on tests.[16]

From their earliest days in school, children of color are thus more likely to experience a factory model of schooling, where children are sorted, controlled, and subjected to standardization to ensure efficiency, preparation for economic roles based on perceived skill, and maintenance of the social order. The high-stakes testing movement that began in the 1990s and continues today has bolstered the factory model, especially in communities of color and low-income communities.[17] The goal of the school-factory is to churn out productive citizens whose behavior matches the white, middle-class, nondisabled standards of the greater society and who therefore can contribute economically. Anyone who cannot fit this mold is considered disposable.

McDermott, Goldman, and Varenne (2006) argue that this rigid, efficiency-driven, "compulsively competitive" culture of schooling is what leads to children of color being disproportionately identified for special education eligibility.[18] They explain, "American education is well-organized to make hierarchy out of differences that can be claimed, however falsely, to be natural, inherent, and potentially consequential in school. . . . The labels are not so much facts about specific children as they are mirrors to what happens in classrooms run by the survival-of-the-show-off-smartest logic of American education."[19] In other words, while we pin labels on children to sort them and maintain hierarchies, the real problem is a racist, ableist culture of schooling that privileges and celebrates the behaviors of a select few while otherizing everyone else.

This picture of the culture of schooling that I am painting is stressful for everyone involved, even children and teachers who have no problem fitting the dominant norms of school. I think very few would describe an environment that is rigid, compliance-oriented, efficient, standards-based, and competitive as "fun." For a neurodivergent child whose brain and body are not designed to operate like the quiet, still, rule-following child that schools aim to mold, conforming to this type of learning environment is impossible and oppressive. While some children with disabilities have access to classrooms and schools that aim to make curricula accessible for their learning styles, most of these children are white, upper class, or both—this is the very "segregation by experience" that Adair and Colegrove warn against.[20]

Building on the work summarized here, I argue that the disproportionate segregation and isolation of children of color with disabilities from their nondisabled peers is a product of an educational system that serves a deep-seated racist and ableist agenda to push out children deemed "deviant" from the culture of schooling. When children do not fit the culture of schooling, they are referred for special education services and then potentially pushed into isolated learning environments. For many, exclusion may not happen right away, but their disability identification puts them at higher risk of isolation in later grades.[21] While the literature on racial disproportionality tends to emphasize the importance of accurate identification, my primary aim is not to determine whether children are appropriately identified for special education.[22] My point in drawing the connection between disproportionate identification and the segregation of children of color with disabilities is to highlight how the practice of exclusion is rooted in racism and ableism embedded *throughout* the special education system. We cannot question exclusionary practice without also questioning how children entered special education to begin with. This book, therefore, though focused on the ultimate segregation and isolation of children of color with disabilities, speaks to systemic injustices that factor into every aspect of special education, as special education referral, identification, and placement all go hand in hand.

(RE)IMAGINING INCLUSION TO REFUSE THE CULTURE OF SCHOOLING

Michael was a fourth grade child with whom I worked as a literacy and math interventionist early in my career. Michael was a Black child who lived with his mother and grandmother in an affordable housing unit close to the school where I worked. His father came to pick Michael up from school once a month or so, but all of the educators' primary communication was with his mother and grandmother. Michael's mother loved his school and all of the educators. She was highly invested in ensuring her child excelled at the school, reaching out to the teachers regularly to get updates on Michael's progress. Michael's mother demonstrated a strong desire to support her son with his academic and social development. Though she often did not have time to try out the strategies and approaches the teachers recommended at home, she listened intently to the ideas and agreed to try them with Michael as often as she could. The one recommendation she did not want to follow year after year was to have Michael evaluated for potential disabilities.

Since kindergarten, Michael's teachers wondered if he might qualify for an IEP. Michael's linguistic development, academic performance, and ability to focus seemed to all of us to be significantly behind his same-age peers. When I worked with him for his interventions, I noticed that Michael was in almost constant motion. His eye gaze shifted around the room; he seemed to look everywhere but the texts we were reading as a group. Although he was placed in a third grade intervention group as a fourth grader, he showed difficulty comprehending the material and keeping up with the younger children in the group, who were also considered "behind" for their grade. I had difficulty supporting Michael in my small-group context, and felt that trying to meet his learning needs in the school's large, inclusive classrooms was too challenging a feat for his teachers. I, therefore, set out on a mission to convince Michael's mother that it was time to get him evaluated for special education.

Over the course of several months, I—with the help of the school administrators and Michael's classroom teachers—convinced Michael's mother to approve an evaluation, despite her strong hesitation to have her child labeled. Michael was ultimately determined eligible for an IEP under the categories of Other Health Impairment (ADHD) and Specific Learning Disabilities. The IEP team later convinced Michael's mother to take him to a pediatrician to see if he would be a good candidate for medication. While she agreed and Michael did indeed start taking medication for ADHD, his mother often told us that she worried he was "no longer himself." The energetic, joyful child she knew now seemed a bit "like a zombie," in her view. Even with the medication and numerous pullout sessions per day, Michael's teachers all felt there was little we could do in our inclusion programs to help Michael excel as a learner. From our perspective, he needed a lot of individualized attention that we could not offer him. Although extremely hesitant, Michael's mother agreed to move Michael to a specialized school that supported children with ADHD and language-based disabilities.

Michael's story is one that often comes to my mind when I think about the systemic exclusion of children of color with disabilities. Early in my career, I taught in settings that served children of color from low-income households, many of whom had an immigrant background. The schools and programs had traditional and narrow definitions for what academic success looked like. Children were expected to behave in compliant and rigid ways, participate in curricula that were white-centric, and develop linguistic and academic skills along trajectories that fit white, middle-class, nondisabled standards. The instruction was highly didactic in nature. Teachers were positioned as all-knowing sages who deposit information into students, who were positioned as empty vessels to be filled. Because the approaches in these school settings fit my own educational experiences as a child, I did not question them.

So, when children like Michael did not fit the expectations that I had of how children should behave and perform in school, I was very quick to assume that they did not belong in inclusive classrooms. I felt they needed help beyond what we were able to provide. In Michael's case, we see how there was room for bias to affect every phase, from his identification for special education eligibility through his eventual separation from his nondisabled peers. We educators pushed for each phase to take place because of our own experiences of challenge, which were influenced by the biased beliefs that we had about how children should exist in school. Never once did we consider other factors in Michael's life that could affect his behavior, nor did we try to implement individualized support for him in his inclusion contexts. Instead, we assumed disability and decided that he needed something beyond what we could offer, thus justifying his exclusion.

What we educators needed to combat the systemic biases that we had internalized was a new way of seeing Michael. Our deficit-based perspectives clouded our vision; all we could see was a child in need of remediation. We also did not have a vision for inclusion that permitted a child like Michael to thrive. In our view, only certain children earned the right to be included and educated alongside their nondisabled peers—children whose ways of being still matched white, nondisabled, middle-class standards. Our mindsets were driven by an exclusionary educational model. We needed to reimagine what inclusion for children of color with disabilities could look like.

What might such revisioning entail? How can we reimagine inclusion for children of color with disabilities—children like Michael or Javier? The main purpose of this book is to offer such a reimagining. It is written for educators like myself or Javier's teacher, who feel like there are no options other than exclusion. I share the story of Michael, despite it being one of the lower moments in my career, because I want to be clear that I too am vulnerable to the exclusionary racist, ableist culture that is pervasive in schooling. I do not write this book from a position of superiority;

rather, I am interrogating systems that have also affected me and my work. Children of color with disabilities are often excluded because a group of adults have internalized cultural ideas that make us believe that these children belong in more restrictive settings. In other words, their bodies are seen through a racist, ableist gaze that tells educators that they do not belong with their white, nondisabled peers. What the field needs is a new vision—an ability to see what feels unimaginable to many.

This book offers such reimagining. I often write "(re)imagining" with the "re" in parentheses because for some, the examples presented in this book may offer a radical perspective on inclusion that they never before considered for children of color with disabilities. That was the case for me when I observed the first truly inclusive classroom I had ever visited. It was two years into my doctoral studies. I had decided to pursue a PhD at Stanford University after teaching in inclusion and special education settings in Connecticut and New York. My original research interests were quite remedial in nature, as my mindset was still dominated by deficit views of children of color and immigrant children with disabilities. Because of my professional experience, as well as my personal experience growing up with family members with disabilities, I assumed that I understood what children of color with disabilities needed: tools to better assimilate to the culture of schooling. This changed when I visited an inclusion classroom in New York City while working as a research assistant on an ethnographic study. The focus of the project was not inclusion, but I happened to be assigned an inclusion classroom to visit for a week. My experience observing the practices in this classroom completely transformed what I knew was even possible for children of color with disabilities. My aim with this book is to offer a similar transformative experience to all who read it.

Drawing from a decade of qualitative, participant observation research in inclusion classrooms in three states—California, Texas, and New York—I present practices that run across inclusive settings where children of color with disabilities are not just included, but are thriving.

The teachers featured in this book interact with children of color with disabilities in ways that *honor* who they are, rather than trying to change who they are. They subsequently create environments and opportunities for children to show their many strengths and capabilities. In so doing, they position the children as belonging with their nondisabled peers.

WHAT DO I MEAN BY *INCLUSION*?

The term *inclusion* is one that is quite complex and contested. In the field of special education, inclusion is tied to federal law and the history of civil rights for children with disabilities. Although states began passing compulsory education laws in the 1800s, state courts upheld the continued exclusion of students with disabilities through the 1960s. It was not until the passage of the Education for All Handicapped Children Act (EAHCA) in 1975—now known as the Individuals with Disabilities in Education Improvement Act (IDEA) 2004—that the federal government mandated that children with disabilities in all states be guaranteed a free and appropriate public education in the least restrictive environment (LRE).[23] The LRE clause is the requirement associated with inclusion, even though the term *inclusion* is not actually found anywhere in IDEA 2004.[24]

The inclusion movement in special education really took off in the 1980s. At that time, there was growing concern around inclusion in the US education system more broadly. Reform advocates—which included educators, researchers, and parents—critiqued the educational system for being monocultural when the US was becoming an increasingly pluralistic and multicultural society. They called for a complete restructuring of schooling to better serve the wide diversity of children in the country. Special education reformists jumped on the momentum of the inclusion movement to advocate for changes in how children with disabilities were seen and served. The inclusion movement thus called for a model of schooling that pulled from general, compensatory, and special education to meet the educational needs of all children. Eventually, however, inclusion became predominantly associated with inclusivity for children with disabilities, and educational placement became the central focus.[25]

The inclusion movement's emphasis on *where* children with disabilities receive their services is not surprising, given that placement in segregated classes or schools was historically the common practice.[26] Physical placement in general education classrooms became a matter of civil rights.[27] Inclusion advocates turned to the LRE mandate as a way to legally justify inclusion, but their counterparts used it to argue against full inclusion, which they believed was not appropriate for children with more severe disabilities or children who had difficulty accessing general education curricula.[28] Such contradictory uses of the law were and continue to be made possible because of the law's ambiguity.[29] In IDEA 2004, the LRE requirement is written as follows:

Each public agency must ensure that—

(i) To the maximum extent appropriate, children with disabilities, including children in public or private institutions or other care facilities, are educated with children who are nondisabled; and
(ii) Special classes, separate schooling, or other removal of children with disabilities from the regular educational environment occurs only if the nature or severity of the disability is such that education in regular classes with the use of supplementary aids and services cannot be achieved satisfactorily.[30]

While on first glance, it may seem as though the law promotes inclusion in the general education classroom as the default placement for children with disabilities, vague language such as "to the maximum extent *appropriate*" and "removal . . . only if . . . education in regular classes . . . cannot be achieved *satisfactorily*" leaves room for educators to justify exclusion. The lack of standardization or specificity around how to determine what is "appropriate" or "satisfactory" means that LRE determinations are subjective.[31] In other words, educators are able to construct "least restrictive" to be whatever they deem fit, making it possible for race- and disability-based biases to influence placement decisions for children of color with disabilities.[32] Because of the LRE clause's vagueness, it has been used to justify the continued exclusion of children with disabilities, specifically children who experience additional, intersecting oppression due to their race, immigration status, language, class, and other characteristics.[33]

Placement decisions are built into a child's IEP. The IEP was considered the centerpiece of the EAHCA of 1975, and it continues to be the critical component of IDEA 2004. It includes the present levels of performance, the disability categories of eligibility, the goals and objectives of the student's educational program, the setting in which the child will receive services, necessary accommodations, how long the child's school year will be (through summer or not), and the evaluation and measurement criteria for determining the child's progress toward goals. Children will first receive an IEP if after a comprehensive multidisciplinary evaluation—conducted by a psychologist and a special education teacher, and/or related service providers—they are determined to qualify for at least one of the thirteen disability categories listed in IDEA 2004. The IEP is meant to be developed in a team meeting that includes educators, specialists, and the child's parents/caregivers.[34]

While the IEP is a legally mandated document that is meant to protect the rights of children with disabilities and their families, the process of developing an IEP is highly subject to bias.[35] These plans are developed by human beings, all of whom bring with them their experiences, beliefs, and worldviews. Ideally, the inclusion of families in the development of IEPs helps to ensure that there is a fuller picture of the child in question, but in my experience, families are rarely included in the actual creation of IEPs. Typically, school personnel come to the IEP meeting with a draft IEP already written, which parents review and agree to (or not). Culturally, racially, and linguistically diverse families are the least likely to be meaningfully included in IEP development because of educators' biases toward the families and barriers such as language.[36] The entire process of developing an IEP, therefore, is subject to bias, including LRE placement decisions.

What IEP teams are considering when making LRE decisions is a continuum of settings that ranges from the general education classroom to segregated, specialized classrooms or schools. The IEP team decides how much time a child with disabilities will spend in the general education classroom (from 0 to 100 percent of the school day) and also in what other settings the child will receive instruction (e.g., resource specialist classes, self-contained special education classrooms, special education schools, etc.). According to federal guidelines, a child is experiencing the highest levels of inclusion when they are in the general education classroom for 80 percent or more of the school day; they experience the lowest levels of inclusion when they are in the general education classroom for 40 percent or less of the school day.[37]

Although inclusion is often thought of in terms of a continuum of educational placement, being in a general education classroom for a majority of the school day does not guarantee least restrictiveness or lack of exclusion.[38] If a child with disabilities who is in the general education classroom for most of the day works one-on-one with a paraprofessional the entire time and never engages with the rest of the class or with the curriculum, it is difficult to say that they are experiencing full inclusion. In the case of Javier described at the beginning of this chapter, we also see how mere placement in a general education setting does not guarantee inclusion. Inclusion advocates, therefore, emphasize that full inclusion is not possible if the general education setting continues to be designed for a singular culture that is nondisabled, white, English-speaking, and middle class.[39] In the way that LRE determinations are currently made, the onus is on the children to show that they can be educated alongside their nondisabled peers. Instead, it should be the responsibility of educators to make environmental changes to their classroom and practice such that children with disabilities and other intersecting identities can also thrive.[40] From this perspective, those who view LRE from the standpoint of a continuum of placement are focusing on the wrong thing. Instead of a continuum of placement, our focus should be on how various general education contexts can be reformed to support all children's learning.

Inclusion is not possible if what children of color with disabilities are being included into continues to be systemically racist and ableist. In fact, the term *inclusion* itself may be troubling, as it positions children of color with disabilities as outsiders who are brought into the insider group's territory. The construct of inclusion is further complicated by the fact that many different models of inclusion are used in schools today. There are classrooms where a few children with disabilities learn alongside their general education peers, with one head teacher and possibly at least one assistant or paraprofessional. There are other classrooms where children with IEPs make up close to half the class and there are two head teachers. In such integrated co-teaching contexts, there is typically one general education head teacher and one special education head teacher. There may also be paraprofessionals supporting the entire class or only one child. Some may also say that if a child with disabilities spends any amount of time at all in a classroom learning alongside general education peers, that child is experiencing inclusion. Others would consider only those cases where a child with disabilities spends 80 percent or more of the day learning alongside general education peers as being inclusive.

The purpose of this book is to advance a vision of schooling where children of color with disabilities are not segregated from their peers but rather are valued as important and equal participants in democratic classrooms designed for all children. The examples that I write about here come from a wide range of contexts that employ different models of inclusion. I am not trying to spotlight a particular model of inclusion; rather, I highlight practices and structures that make it possible for children of color with disabilities to learn alongside their nondisabled peers in meaningful ways. The goal of this book, therefore, is not about promoting specific placement types, although I do ultimately hope to inspire transformative practices that could make possible full inclusion for 100 percent of the school day. Instead, I aim to advance a vision for inclusion that aligns with Artiles and Kozleski's (2007) view: "The basic premise of inclusive school communities is that schools are about belonging, nurturing, and educating all children and youth, regardless of their differences in culture, gender, language, ability, class, and ethnicity."[41] I look at inclusion in terms of belonging—how do educators nurture or deny a sense of belonging for the children of color with disabilities included in their classrooms? Children with disabilities who learn alongside their nondisabled peers for 100 percent of the school day can still experience exclusion if they do not have a sense of belonging. My aim is to show how true full inclusion is made possible by educators who are committed to building democratic classrooms where all children belong.

THE EVIDENCE BASE AND ORGANIZATION OF THIS BOOK

The examples of inclusive practice described in this book come from a decade of qualitative research in schools and classrooms in three states: California, Texas, and New York. All the settings are in urban districts that predominantly serve students of color from low-income backgrounds and have high numbers of multilingual learners. Each research project that I draw from involved ethnographic, participant observation methods in elementary schools serving large populations of children of color with disabilities. Across these projects, I partnered with forty-nine teachers in thirty-four classrooms. All the classrooms were considered inclusion classrooms, though the models for inclusion varied. Some were integrated, co-teaching classrooms where up to 40 percent of the children had IEPs, while others were general education classrooms with one head teacher, which had a handful of children with IEPs. Special education services were provided to children through a variety of means, including push-in services, consultation with the general education teacher, pullout services, co-teaching, and more.

For each project, I collected data on the educational experiences of children of color with disabilities in these inclusive contexts. The children predominantly had Black, Latinx, and Asian racial backgrounds. Many of the children were also from immigrant families and labeled as "English learners." Data collection involved writing field notes from observations in the classroom; interviewing educators (including classroom teachers, administrators, and support personnel), with all the interviews recorded and later transcribed; and compiling documents and other artifacts relevant to the observations (e.g., work samples, student assessment data, etc.). For some projects, I also interviewed parents about their children's educational trajectories.

Across these many contexts, I observed a range of practices that either promoted or inhibited belonging for children of color with disabilities. While gathering data over the years, I became interested in understanding more deeply *how* teachers foster belonging for children of color with disabilities. My underlying theory is that exclusion can be prevented if educators know how to cultivate communities of belonging in their inclusive classrooms. I thus revisited the data from my various projects to specifically examine the practices enacted in inclusive settings that led to exclusion or belonging.

In my analysis, I focused on individual interactions among educators and children, among children themselves, and between children and materials. Annamma and Morrison (2018) explain that liberatory pedagogy for children of color with disabilities is possible only when educators cease to view their children of color with disabilities through a deficit lens.[42] Only then are they able to create more expansive opportunities for children that disrupt the status quo and explore children's "multidimensional assets."[43] Teachers' practices, therefore, reflect their ontological and epistemological orientations—what do the teachers believe about the ways of being (ontology) and knowing (epistemology) in children of color with disabilities? When analyzing my data from inclusion classrooms, I focused on interactions because it is in the ways that individuals interact with each other and with the world around them that ontology and epistemology are revealed.

For example, if a teacher believes that how a child moves his or her body is deficient, that teacher might physically maneuver the child to get the child to move in a particular way (e.g., the hand-over-hand practice common in special education where an adult will put a hand over a child's and move the child's hand in the way that the adult desires), or the teacher might enact disciplinary measures as a form of negative reinforcement to deter undesired behaviors (e.g., excluding a child from an activity because the body is "not safe"). On the other hand, if a teacher sees the child's movements as an expression of self that is not undesirable or requiring change, but rather should be accepted and celebrated, the teacher might look for ways to support the child's physical expressions. Focusing on interactions between people, as well as between people and materials, allows me to see the many small ways in which educators might enact a liberatory or exclusionary approach to inclusion.

In this book, I draw on numerous interactions to present a reimagining of inclusion that would advance belonging and liberation for children of color with disabilities. In part I, "What Are We (Re)Imagining and How?" I lay the foundation for my argument that to truly change the pattern of exclusion that children of color with disabilities continue to experience, we must shift inclusive practices away from approaches that adhere to the medical model of disability that predominates special education.[44] In the medical model, disability is regarded as a problem to be "fixed" or "cured" in an individual. When educators view disability through this lens, the practices that they enact are interventionist in nature.[45] I describe what these medical model–aligned approaches look like to make visible the collusive, interdependent, and often invisible ways that ableism and racism work together to oppress children of color with disabilities in inclusion classrooms. Through examples from the field, I show how interventionist practices are used to enact erasure against children of color with disabilities. I illuminate specific interactions and pedagogical moves that work to force conformity to a dominant culture of schooling that is rooted in nondisabled whiteness. I also show how these medical model approaches help educators build a case for the exclusion of children of color with disabilities. This leads to the children being pushed out of inclusion classrooms and moved into more restrictive, isolated settings.

I then provide a summary of the two primary theories guiding this book: Disability Critical Race Studies (DisCrit) and a DisCrit Classroom Ecology.[46] DisCrit and DisCrit Classroom Ecology were developed in response to the hypermedicalized, normalizing oppressions enacted on individuals of color with disabilities. They offer a framework for both critically assessing status quo practices and reimagining what transformation of schooling for children of color with disabilities might entail. I aim to concretize these theories by demonstrating what DisCrit-aligned, transformational inclusive practices actually look like. In this first section, I also describe the evidence for the text, specifically explaining who the educators and children featured in the text are and why their inclusive practices are being highlighted.

The second and third sections draw from examples from inclusion classrooms to operationalize two components of a DisCrit Classroom Ecology: DisCrit Pedagogy and DisCrit Solidarity. The educators spotlighted in these sections are, in my view, rare teachers whose approaches I elevate to support our collective reimagining of inclusive pedagogy. Section II, "(Re)Imagining toward DisCrit Pedagogy in Inclusion Classrooms," focuses on DisCrit Pedgagogy, which requires an embodiment of expansive practices that aim to build on and showcase the many assets of children of color with disabilities.[47] In this section, I detail specific pedagogical moves that educators make. I analyze interactions among teachers and children, among children, and between children and materials to illuminate the pedagogical practices in transformational, inclusive

DisCrit classroom ecologies. The pedagogical moves that I highlight fall under the following themes: *responding with respect, not restriction*; *making room for the unexpected*; and *centering inquiry*. Each theme is described in its own chapter to show the many ways that educators can enact a pedagogy that celebrates the various gifts and assets that children of color with disabilities bring with them into the inclusion classroom.

In section III, "(Re)Imagining toward DisCrit Solidarity in Inclusion Classrooms," I operationalize what DisCrit Solidarity looks like in inclusion classrooms. DisCrit Solidarity is a critical element of a DisCrit Classroom Ecology because of the status quo tendency to punish, surveil, and restrain the behaviors of children of color with disabilities. Educators who enact DisCrit Solidarity are able to recognize and celebrate the gifts of resistance that children of color with disabilities express.[48] It is when teachers reject the deficit lens often applied to children of color with disabilities that they can develop authentic solidarity and relationship with the students.[49] In this section of the book, I provide concrete examples of how teachers engage in acts of solidarity with their students of color with disabilities. The two themes that these acts fall under are *recognizing the gifts of resistance* and *centering relationships.*

My aim with this book is to share practices that run across inclusive settings where children of color with disabilities are not just included, but thriving. The featured teachers interact with children of color with disabilities in ways that honor who they are, rather than trying to change who they are. They subsequently create environments and opportunities for children to show their many strengths and capabilities. In so doing, the educators enact pedagogies of belonging that advance democracy is their inclusive classrooms.

I

What Are We (Re)Imagining, and How?

1

Justifying Exclusion Through the Medical Model of Disability

THE PRACTICE OF SEGREGATING children of color with disabilities from their nondisabled peers stems from the medical model of disability that is pervasive in US schools. Disability studies scholars distinguish between several models of disability, one of which is the medical model, which continues to be the predominant model of disability in society today.[1] The notion of the medical model was first developed in the field of psychiatry in the 1950s, when Dr. Thomas Szasz criticized his own field for pathologizing human emotion and behaviors. He accused psychiatrists of creating diseases of the mind to enforce social order.[2] In the 1980s and 1990s, as the field of disability studies was developing and gaining traction, a subset of special education practitioners and researchers began identifying and questioning the dominance of the medical model of disability in schools.[3]

In the medical model, disability is framed as a problem that exists within an individual, which needs to be remediated or cured through intervention and treatment.[4] The medical model is strongly normative, where individuals are labeled as having disabilities because they do not behave in ways deemed "normal." Their so-called abnormalities are thus seen as undesirable, and the purpose of educational intervention is to eradicate the unwanted behaviors and bring the individual closer to the norm.[5] In special education, the concern is often about ensuring that the disabled student can later become a functioning member of society. Treatments then become focused on helping the student fit the norms of society rather than trying to adjust the environment to suit the student.

Removing children with disabilities from general education contexts is thus used as a means of "fixing" or "curing" them until they are ready to rejoin the nondisabled community.[6] The likelihood that children with disabilities who are isolated from their nondisabled peers will later experience inclusion, however, is quite small. Research indicates that children with disabilities are only more likely to experience segregated placement as they move into upper grades, and Black students with disabilities experience the least inclusion over time.[7] Nationwide, children considered to have the most severe disabilities have not seen increases in the time they are included in general education settings with nondisabled peers for the last decade.[8] This is especially the case for children of color with more severe disabilities across races, who are more likely to be placed in segregated contexts than are their white peers.[9]

Physical removal from an inclusive or general education context is not the only form of intervention used in the medical model in schools. Any practice meant to force children with disabilities to conform to the norm is considered a pathologizing, interventionist approach. Something as seemingly benign as a behavior chart rewards children for compliance and punishes them for noncompliance in an effort to train them to internalize the behavior expectations and culture of school.[10] Behavior charts are pathologizing and interventionist because they isolate undesirable behaviors with the aim of extracting them, much as a medical doctor identifies an illness and treats it to remove it from a patient's body.

Educational practices that align with the medical model of disability, therefore, are designed to find problems within children and remove or "fix" those problems through interventions that replace the undesired behaviors with normative, desired ones.

The pervasiveness of the medical model of disability can be linked to the origins of special education as a field. When the Education for All Handicapped Children Act (EAHCA) was passed in 1975, it was a civil rights response to the perpetual, often legalized exclusion of children with disabilities from the entire education system.[11] As the existence of special education was in question, special education teachers were in the position of needing to justify their profession from the start. The medical model of disability, therefore, served the purpose of legitimating special education by positioning special education teachers as professionals who could help to rid our society of the supposed "deviance" that children with disabilities showed. In the medical model, then, there exists a power dynamic between special education professionals and children with disabilities. Educators are the ones who rehabilitate or cure students, who are the ones who need to be cured.[12] This power dynamic makes it possible for educators to enact dehumanizing behavior replacement or reduction plans centered on reinforcement, punishment, and isolation.[13]

It is important to note that my critique of the medical model of disability must not be mistaken for a critique of the field of medicine as a whole. Medical advances have served important purposes in addressing the pain and suffering associated with the vast array of impairments with which disabled individuals live. What I mean to trouble is an orientation toward thinking about and interacting with human variation that is pathologizing and dehumanizing—an approach to disability where human beings are treated as problems to be fixed rather than choosing to examine society for its discriminatory flaws. I also do not mean to suggest that there is no place for interventions and educational strategies to support the learning and development of children of color with disabilities. My intent is to question those practices that serve the purpose of trying to force conformity into a mythological "normal"—practices that have their roots in the legacy of eugenics and a belief that certain ways of being are unworthy of belonging in our society.[14] This stance of erasure is at the heart of the medical model of disability.

When you couple the medical model of disability with the cultural assimilationist agenda of schooling, it is easily apparent how children of color with disabilities are particularly stigmatized and oppressed. Paris (2012) explains that schools are dominated by deficit approaches to teaching and learning that position the knowledges, cultures, and languages of communities of color as deficiencies to overcome. Children are expected to fit white, middle-class norms. Their own community assets and ways of being are seen as unworthy. As Paris puts it, "The goal of deficit approaches was to eradicate the linguistic, literate, and cultural practices many students of color brought from their homes and communities and to replace them with what were viewed as superior practices."[15] Just as the medical model of disability advances pathologizing, rehabilitative, or curative treatments, deficit approaches to teaching and learning aim to force assimilation and conformity to whiteness for children of color.

Children of color with disabilities, therefore, experience erasure in multiple forms, their intersecting identities viewed as deficits that inhibit their ability to perform and exist in ways deemed desirable in the US education system. Children of color with disabilities are then subjected to the most extreme forms of isolation, exclusion, rehabilitation, and intervention. In my work in inclusion classrooms, I have found that there are two prevailing ways that educators interact with children of color with disabilities to restrict, control, and ultimately exclude them: restricting the body, and restricting language and meaning-making. These restrictions contribute to a discourse surrounding individual children of color with disabilities that justifies their removal from inclusive settings.

RESTRICTING THE BODIES OF CHILDREN OF COLOR WITH DISABILITIES

It is 12:30 p.m. sharp. The children in Ms. Tannenbaum and Mr. Becker's second-grade class are lined up against the wall outside their classroom. Children are called three at a time to put their lunch boxes and jackets in their hallway cubbies and then enter the classroom. Ms. Tannenbaum enters the classroom with the first group of children called and directs them to their desks. She sets a timer hanging on the wall for five minutes. As children come into the classroom three at a time, they follow Ms. Tannenbaum's instructions to walk straight to their desks, sit down, pull out a workbook and pencil, and begin working on their assigned math problems.

Jeremiah, the only Black child in the classroom and one of eight students with individualized education programs (IEPs), walks into the classroom with a bit of a dance in his step. With the hood from his red sweatshirt up over his head, Jeremiah sways his shoulders and steps to a beat that only he seems to hear. He saunters toward his desk, pausing every few steps to give his shoulders a shake.

Ms. Tannenbaum sees Jeremiah and walks over to him saying in a stern tone, "No. Try again. Your body is not being safe."

"What?" Jeremiah looks at his teacher with a surprised expression on his face.

"You have an unsafe body," Ms. Tannenbaum says. She holds Jeremiah by the shoulders to turn him around so he is facing the classroom door. She starts to walk him out of the classroom when Jeremiah pushes her hands off of him.

"What did I do?" he asks. "Don't touch me!"

"No. Try again. Your body is not being safe." Ms. Tannenbaum holds onto Jeremiah's arm and pulls him out of the classroom as he wrestles to get free from her grasp. Mr. Becker then enters the room to take Ms. Tannenbaum's place of directing the class's transition while

> Ms. Tannenbaum and Jeremiah exit the classroom. Mr. Becker closes the door. As the rest of the class sits quietly at their desks, independently working in their math workbooks, we can hear Jeremiah shouting in the hallway. From the small classroom door window, we see glimpses of Jeremiah kicking and hitting Ms. Tannenbaum. Eventually, two administrators come and take Jeremiah away as he kicks and screams.

This scene is emblematic of interactions that Jeremiah regularly had with his teachers in his second-grade inclusion classroom. Later, in my interview with Jeremiah's teachers, Ms. Tannenbaum reflected on this moment and said, "His body can really be unsafe." When I asked her to elaborate, she told me, "I don't think you could see, but in the hallway he was kicking me, like jump kicks. He started pulling things off the wall and out of cubbies. He was like a tornado. He even hit one of his peers." When I asked Ms. Tannenbaum to tell me more about how Jeremiah's "body was unsafe" when he walked into the classroom, she said, "So that's why we have everyone walk straight to their desks when they walk in. We don't want anyone to be unsafe, especially with our group this year. Anything can set them off and they'll lose control. So when Jeremiah walked in like that, I just knew something was going to happen, and it did."

Jeremiah's experience in his inclusion classroom reflects two common ways that children of color with disabilities can experience medical model–aligned restriction of their bodies: narrow definitions of appropriate movement, and restraint and removal in response to movement deemed inappropriate. Eight-year-old Jeremiah was enrolled in an inclusion classroom that had a co-teaching model. Ms. Tannenbaum was the special education teacher and Mr. Becker was the general education teacher, and the two shared full instructional responsibility. The class was racially diverse, mostly comprised of children from white, Asian, and Latinx racial backgrounds. As noted previously, Jeremiah was the only Black child and one of only eight children with IEPs in the class; his IEP was for Other Health Impairment (ADHD) and Emotional Behavior Disorder.

Jeremiah and his classmates all experienced bodily restrictions due to narrow definitions of appropriate movement. His teachers set the expectation that the children must move their bodies in particular ways and within particular time frames. During the moment of transition described here, children were to walk quickly and in an orderly fashion, at set times, to put away their items, move to their desks, take out work, and engage with materials. The characterization of Jeremiah's body as "unsafe" shows just how narrow the expectations were around appropriate movement in this classroom. When he walked into the room with a dance in his step, his body was read as dangerous and deviant, with the potential to set off uncontrollable behavior among the whole class.

The teachers' response to Jeremiah's "undesirable" movements was an enactment of the second type of bodily restriction—restraint and removal. The teacher physically restrained Jeremiah, holding him by the shoulders or the arm and moving him toward the classroom door to have him reattempt entering the classroom in an "appropriate" manner. When he physically expressed his discomfort with this restraint, pushing and pulling away from his teacher, he was removed from the classroom and punished. Interestingly, it was not until Jeremiah experienced restraint and removal that he actually moved his body in ways that could cause harm to himself or others. The restriction of his body set off a vicious cycle that led to Jeremiah responding in ways that further justified his restraint and removal.

Such restrictions on children's bodies are manifestations of the medical model of disability because they are strongly normative. They are interventions aimed at "curing" individuals of unwanted physical movement to ensure conformity to a norm. In the inclusion classrooms that I have observed, restriction of bodies follows a general sequence that encompasses the two types of restriction seen in Jeremiah's case. First, children's movements are controlled using a range of strategies designed to enforce desired behaviors. These strategies include verbal redirection, behavior charts, class rules or norms, and, for children with disabilities, sometimes support from a one-on-one paraprofessional who verbally or physically assists the child with meeting bodily expectations. The phrase "your body is not being safe" is one of the most common redirections I've heard in classrooms, particularly with children of color with disabilities. While the phrase is sometimes used to indicate that the child in question could potentially get hurt, often it is used out of fear that the child will harm others, thus positioning the child as dangerous and reinforcing racial stereotypes. All these normative strategies have the effect of otherizing children with disabilities whose ways of being may not match the expectations of the classroom.

If a child is not conforming to the narrow definition of appropriate movement and a range of strategies have been tried, then practices of restraint and removal are attempted. Restraint and removal fall along a spectrum of extremity. Increasingly extreme practices are applied when a child does not exhibit the desired physical behaviors for longer periods. One kindergartner, Sebastian, is a child for whom this gradual progression of increasingly intense restraint and removal occurred. He was enrolled in an inclusion classroom that had twenty-seven other kindergartners and three teachers. The children were all either Latinx or Black, and there were ten children with IEPs. Sebastian was of Ecuadorian descent; his family had emigrated to the US a few years before he was born. He had an IEP for Speech or Language Impairment, although his teachers suspected that other disability categories might be added to his IEP once the district did another full evaluation of him for his triannual IEP meeting in the following year.

Sebastian was enrolled in a school that emphasized orderly, rigid behavior management. A key way that behavioral expectations were enforced was through a digital app that allowed teachers to administer points to individual children whenever they met certain expectations. If a child transitioned quickly and quietly, he or she got a point. If a child was seated on the rug with legs crossed and eyes on the teacher, he or she got a point. If a child raised a hand to answer a question, he or she got a point. Essentially, any time that children followed directions and moved their bodies in ways deemed desirable in school, they received a point on the app. The school also tracked each classroom's point accumulation and gave out prizes to individual children, as well as entire classrooms, each month based on the number of points they accrued.

Sebastian showed difficulty with adhering to the norms reinforced by this medical model–aligned, behaviorist point system. In his classroom, stern verbal redirection was another way that expectations were reinforced. Each day as I approached Sebastian's classroom, from down the hallway I could hear his name being called by stern voices reminding him of behavioral expectations or reprimanding him. When I first met Sebastian, the first thing I noticed was that he seemed to have a permanent smile on his face. He approached each task in the classroom with tremendous vigor and enthusiasm. Sometimes his verve would manifest in sudden, unexpected, high-pitched shrieks coupled with a thrusting forward of his arms. When sitting on the rug, he often lifted his entire body upward as he made declarations. "Quiet," "Stop," "Sit down on your bottom," and "Wait your turn" were directives that teachers frequently used with Sebastian.

His teachers described Sebastian as "distracting to others" and a child who "does not have self-control of his body." One teacher said that he was a child she always had to watch. She went on to say:

> Sebastian can sometimes walk away and I won't pay any mind. Because it's gonna cause a bigger distraction by me stopping, right? And then other times I see him doing things and I'm like, well, that bookshelf is going to fall on top of you. So, you know, we cannot continue on with that . . . He has a lot of outside forces that don't support him. And so coming in here, it's like he expects you to behave the same way with him as at home. When you don't, it's like, "Oh, well." [*makes an explosion gesture with her hands and a corresponding explosion sound*]

Perhaps because the teachers felt that they needed to redirect and watch Sebastian constantly, he was assigned a table seat that was separate from the rest of the class. Whenever the children were instructed to go to their tables, Sebastian went to the back corner of the room to a table tucked away next to the classroom library. There, he sat in a chair that was surrounded on three sides by a wall, a bookshelf, and the table. Although there were other seats at the table, Sebastian sat there alone, isolated from the rest of the class, whose tables were on the other side of the room. If a child chose to sit at Sebastian's table for independent work time, a teacher would tell the child to sit elsewhere.

Confined to his little corner of the room, Sebastian frequently moved his body in big, athletic ways when his teachers were not looking. He would leapfrog back and forth over his chair, lie with his back on the chair to get into a wheelbarrow pose, find objects around him to toss in the air and catch, and other activities. When teachers saw him, they would tell Sebastian to "sit properly in [his] seat" or "You're showing me you need a break. Shall we call [the assistant principal] to come get you?" Peers might also notice Sebastian and point his behavior out to teachers, who would then reprimand him.

Each day that I observed in Sebastian's classroom, he would experience full removal from the classroom at some point. For example, take the following scene from one observation:

> The children gather on the rug for a read-aloud. Sebastian is seated toward the back of the meeting area, sitting on his knees so he can see the teacher and the book above his peers' heads. The teacher leads the children in a call-and-response exercise, where she reads a line and the children repeat after her. As this activity unfolds, Sebastian slowly scoots his way up to the front of the room, his enthusiasm seeming to launch him forward closer to the book as he recites each line. A few times, he repeats after the teacher in a loud voice. The teacher turns to

Sebastian each time and says, "You don't need to be shouting" or "Stop calling out."

When he makes it all the way to the front of the room and is seated directly in front of the teacher, she looks down at him and says, "What—how did you get here?" The teacher tells Sebastian to go back to his spot at the back of the rug. He turns around and scoots himself back toward his original spot, but then starts to make his way toward a table next to the rug. Once there, he gets up, grabs a chair, and sits in it, still facing the teacher and the read-aloud book. The teacher sees this and says, "Unh unh, no, go back to your spot please." Sebastian stands up and walks to his original spot. He is no longer facing the teacher and book, but instead fiddles with something hanging on the shelf behind him.

After some group discussion about the text, the teacher sends the children to their tables to begin working on a worksheet about the read-aloud. Sebastian gets up and begins skipping and hopping to his seat. "Sebastian, calm down," one teacher says, prompting him to stop his motions and instead walk steadily to his corner table. As the children work on their task, the teachers circulate the room and check in with children individually. Sebastian, however, is left alone for the first ten minutes of the work time. After fiddling with his pencil and drawing on his paper for some time, Sebastian begins flinging his body side to side in his chair, exclaiming "Whoa," as he lets his torso fall to the ground, and then picks himself up to move the other way.

When one teacher sees what Sebastian is doing, she tells him to move to a round table in the dramatic play area of the room, further separated from his classmates. Another teacher comes over to him and reviews a chart that the adults are using to track Sebastian's behavior. He is told that he already had two strikes for the day and needs five more stickers in order to earn a prize. Sebastian is then left alone for the remainder of the work time.

> At the end of this literacy block, it is time to transition to snack. A child who is passing out milk drops a carton of milk. As he goes to get paper towels, another child who is passing out pretzels slips on the milk and falls. Sebastian sees this, runs over, and begins sliding around in the milk, also falling from the slipperiness. A teacher goes over to Sebastian, lifts him up by the arm, and says, "This is strike three. You need a break." This teacher walks Sebastian out of the classroom, holding him by the arm, and takes him to the assistant principal's office.

This scene with Sebastian shows how one child of color with disabilities moved through a series of increasingly restrictive forms of restraint and removal. Sebastian's way of moving and vocalizing did not fit the tightly defined norms around appropriate behavior in his classroom. Along with the behavioristic reinforcers used for all children in the class, Sebastian had his own individual behavior tracker, which was meant to further enforce conformity with the classroom's norm. As a result, Sebastian's behaviors were hypersurveilled.

His isolated seating was the first form of restraint and removal that Sebastian experienced. He was physically restricted by the tight corner he was placed in, surrounded on three sides so he could not move very much. When he tried to move out of his designated spot on the rug, he was again restricted and told to move back to his place. Sitting in a chair was also not an option for him. The more Sebastian was restrained from moving in ways that he desired, the more he disengaged from the classroom's activities. As he found ways to subversively move his body in his own way, he experienced further restraint. He was given strikes on his behavior tracker, was moved to yet another, more isolated table in the room, and eventually was pushed out of the classroom for a period of time. While I did not observe Sebastian's classroom long enough to know what transpired for him over the longer term, for many children of color with disabilities, repeatedly experiencing this cycle of normative, medical model restriction leads to ultimate segregation into specialized classrooms or schools, separated from their nondisabled peers.

ENFLESHMENT AND BIOPOWER: THEORETICAL FRAMES FOR UNDERSTANDING THE BODILY RESTRICTION OF CHILDREN OF COLOR WITH DISABILITIES

The sequence of bodily restriction that Jeremiah, Sebastian, and so many other children of color with disabilities experience follows Peter McLaren's theory of *enfleshment* and Michel Foucault's theory of *biopower.* McLaren is an educational sociologist credited as being one of the leading architects of critical pedagogy—a "framework of liberation of the oppressed from forces and relations of exploitation."[16] In his work, he calls for curricula and pedagogies that foster revolutionary critical knowledge-making, leading to the transformation of unjust social relations and structures.[17] In McLaren's view, critical pedagogy is necessary to undo the cultural indoctrination that occurs in school, whereby children are taught a way of being that perpetuates social injustice. This learning of school culture is not just intellectual, it is physically embodied. In his article, "Schooling the Postmodern Body: Critical Pedagogy and the Politics of Enfleshment," McClaren explains that dominant cultural practices of schools become embedded in the flesh. Our bodies learn expected ways of being, as "we are taught to think about our bodies and how to experience our bodies."[18]

McLaren's theory of *enfleshment* connects with the neoliberal French philosopher Michel Foucault's theory of *biopower.* In the last few decades, educational researchers have drawn on Foucauldian theories in their analyses of power relations in school practice and policy.[19] One such theory is the concept of *biopower.* Foucault's *biopower* helps explain how the *enfleshment* that McLaren describes occurs. *Biopower* is the process, while *enfleshment* is the outcome. In his theory of *biopower,* Foucault argues that those in power subjugate those without power by using physical or ideological force to turn them into what he calls "docile bodies"—individuals who behave in ways that those in power desire. In school, docile bodies would be children who are appropriately enfleshed to act in their bodies as they are told to behave.

According to Foucault, there are three means of correct training or subjection in *biopower*:

(1) *Hierarchical observation,* which is when those in authority surveille those without power.
(2) *Normalizing judgment,* which is the process of comparing and ranking individuals against a norm.
(3) *The examination,* which is an analysis of some sort that ultimately determines who is a docile body and who is an undocile body that must be removed.

All of these processes serve to enflesh docile body norms into the bodies of children in school.[20]

We can see how enfleshment and biopower play out in the case of Danny, another child for whom medical model–aligned restriction of the body led to his experiencing exclusion. When I observed Danny's classroom, he was a Chinese immigrant fifth grader with an IEP for Autism and Specific Learning Disabilities enrolled in a Cantonese-English dual immersion classroom. There were thirty-three children in his class—five of whom had IEPs—and one teacher. The school had just rolled out a Positive Behavior Interventions and Supports (PBIS) system, where children and entire classrooms earned tickets that could be traded for prizes at set times throughout the year. As the name indicates, the goal of PBIS is to teach and reinforce positive or desired behaviors, while intervening with inappropriate or undesired behaviors to manage and eventually eradicate them. PBIS thus aligns with the medical model of disability due to its normative aims. The behaviors that were considered desirable at Danny's school included walking quietly in a straight line with hands clasped behind the back, answering adults or responding to their directions immediately, sitting with crossed legs and facing the teacher on the rug or sitting with hands clasped on the desk while facing the teacher, and speaking only when directed to do so.

The rigid behavior norms in Danny's school seemed to be difficult for many children to adhere to, regardless of whether they had a disability. However, it was children with disabilities related to behavior, such as Attention Deficit Hyperactivity Disorder (ADHD), Emotional Disturbance, Autism, and Intellectual Disabilities, who were most often told to stand in a corner facing the wall for a time-out, go to the principal's office, meet with the teacher during recess, and other commonly used approaches for punishing unwanted behavior. They were also the children least likely to receive tickets and corresponding rewards. Danny was one such child. He was often reprimanded for his behavior and hardly ever received tickets.

Danny engaged in many physical behaviors that were of concern to his educators. The report that his teacher submitted to his special education teacher for his annual IEP meeting described Danny as follows:

> Isolated, negative, sudden comments which is out of context, talking to self, not willing (avoid) to participate, not focused in class, often chooses activities he prefers, unwilling to work with others, doesn't play with others during recess, often observes ants/insects, complains about being bullied/teased, sensitive.

While Danny's fifth-grade teacher identified many behaviors, several were tied directly to his physical body, such as where he did or did not focus his attention, as well as his self-imposed physical separation from peers. Danny's previous teachers conveyed additional concerns about his physicality in his report cards. These concerns were related to how he expressed negative emotions. For example:

- "Danny needs to work on dealing with frustrations and disappointments as he has a hard time accepting facts when it does not come out the way he expects. He needs to try his best at everything instead of becoming discouraged and upset" (first-grade report card).

- "Danny is eager to participate in class discussions, but he needs to raise his hand and wait to be called on when he wants to share information. He also needs to learn how to keep his hands and feet to himself, along with articulating his feelings in a calm manner when he feels wronged" (third-grade report card).
- "Danny has been displaying some anger and has a hard time making friends with others" (fourth-grade report card).

I observed Danny show these various behaviors when I visited his classroom. I noticed that he did not engage in partner or group tasks; he sat on his own at his desk, refusing to move or change his positioning to interact with others. His classmates also did not make any attempts to engage him unless their teacher directed them to do so. During whole group lessons, Danny directed his attention to things around the room or in his desk that were not related to the instruction. Once during a math lesson, the students were working on multiplying fractions using what was called the "area model." The session consisted of three parts: a mini-lesson, paired poster creations, and a gallery walk. For one hour, while his peers pulled out their workbooks, solved problems, created posters, and judged each other's work, Danny sat in his chair and alternated between pulling at his eyelashes and cutting his jeans with scissors. Whenever his teacher came over to instruct Danny to do his work, he sat still, faced forward, and did not respond to her.

Although Danny did not seem to engage much with the work of his classroom, he also did not enjoy the process of being pulled out for special education services. It was when he was pulled out of the classroom by the resource room teacher that I most often observed Danny display the anger and frustration that his previous teachers had noted. For example, during one observation of a resource room session, the following ensued:

> Danny was in the resource room sitting at a small table across from his resource room teacher, Ms. Li. Ms. Li had given Danny a sheet with

sentences on them to practice his reading fluency. About five minutes into their session, Danny pounded his fists on the table and exclaimed, "This is taking forever! It's almost 10 o'clock! I still have a lot of work to do, man! Six worksheets of classroom!" Danny started rubbing the eraser against his finger. Then he took an eraser and began stabbing it with his pencil. Ms. Li took the eraser from him. As they continued reading, Danny paused periodically to pound his fists on the table and shout a comment related to the work taking a long time and his wanting to return to the classroom to complete his "six worksheets." We later learned that the "sheets" Danny wanted to work on were his homework assignments that he did during class time so he wouldn't have to do them at home.

The sentences Danny read became increasingly difficult. After he struggled to read one sentence, Danny said, "This is getting harder, man! I bet you could barely read them yourself."

Ms. Li said, "If you have trouble reading a word, you can just skip it and move on to the next one."

Danny said, "I don't have trouble. This is pretty dumb." He then leaned his chair far back, looking as though he might fall. Ms. Li told him to lean forward so he wouldn't hurt himself. "I need to come back, man. I'm missing a ton of work, man." Then he started pounding his fist on the table and shouted, "I need to go!" He lifted his fists and shook them in the air in frustration. Then he took the eraser and his pencil and began poking holes into the eraser over and over.

Ms. Li asked if he wanted to drink some water or go to the restroom. Danny shouted, "No! Not until recess time." He continued to stab the eraser with his pencil. Then the lead fell out of his mechanical pencil and he shouted, "No!"

Ms. Li told him he could put the lead back in. Danny put the lead into the pencil and then slowly pumped the lead from the mechanical pencil into an eraser. "I'm inject a needle," he said. "Slowly goes a needle." This action seemed to calm Danny for a moment.

> Ms. Li prompted him to continue reading the sentences. "Aww, man! I have the most homework in the world!" Then he shouted, "I don't wanna do this, man!" as he stabbed his pencil into the paper really hard.
>
> Ms. Li told Danny that she had about twenty more minutes with him. She told him that he could either do it now or later. "I wanna get out!" he shouted. "I don't want to do. I want to do another time!" Then Danny got up out of his chair and ran toward the door. Ms. Li called him back. He walked back but then grabbed a hold of his chair and slammed it down onto the ground.
>
> Ms. Li said, "I can get you after lunch."
>
> Danny shouted, "I don't want to do this! Monday's where there's a ton of classwork. You always pull me when there's a ton of classwork." Ms. Li then sent him back to his class.

Danny frequently expressed frustration about being pulled out of his classroom to go to the resource room. His emotions intensified when the work during these pullout sessions felt challenging. Once a week, he was pulled out to do math work with a group of second-grade children. He often argued with one of the second-grade children, who teased Danny when he had difficulty with math problems. One day, Ms. Li told me that Danny had jump-kicked the second grader and was sent to the principal's office. He was then recommended for counseling, which was one more reason for Danny to get pulled out of his classroom.

As the year went on, Danny's teacher became increasingly concerned about his academic and social-emotional development. He was going to be transitioning to middle school at the end of fifth grade. She was concerned about his ability to meet the demands of middle school. As she shared in an interview with me:

> His previous teachers didn't see his issues as anything too severe. Now that he is in fifth grade and has to do higher-level things, I am able to see more problems that he is having. I think he has a very creative side

> of him, but he is special, very unique in certain ways in terms of behavior. And he is having some specific needs that have to be supported by other services or maybe more intensive, one-on-one kind of teaching instead of just being in a class of thirty-something students with whole group instructions. I think it's not actually beneficial for him to be in this kind of setting.

Danny's classroom teacher and the resource specialist teacher collected data documenting Danny's behavior, as well as his academic growth. They ultimately determined that he was too far behind grade level across subject areas to move on to middle school without more intensive support than what he received in elementary school.

At Danny's IEP meeting at the end of the schoolyear, the IEP team met with a special education teacher from the middle school that Danny was going to attend the following year. The group decided that Danny would receive most of his instructional blocks in specialized classes designed for children with disabilities. He would join nondisabled peers for electives, lunch, and extracurricular activities. Although Danny's mother agreed to this plan, she told me later in an interview through a Cantonese-English translator, "His behavior is not that serious. I hope he will listen more when he goes to middle school. And that he can communicate with friends. But I want them to do what needs to be done. At least with this plan, when he doesn't know something, a special person will help him." Danny's mother seemed a bit hesitant about her son being separated from nondisabled peers for so much of the day, but she also agreed to the plan because she wanted her child to get the support that the professionals felt he needed.

In Danny's case, we see *enfleshment* enacted through the rigid behavioral expectations at his school, which were enforced through PBIS. When children deviated from these expectations, as Danny often did, they experienced restraint and removal. Danny was thus subjected to the *hierarchical observation* and *normalization* that Foucault describes in his theory of biopower. He was watched by the adults at the school, compared to the norms established by the new PBIS, and then given interventions when he did not meet those norms. Even after being pulled out regularly for these interventions, Danny was not able to be subjugated into a "docile body." The teachers then moved to the *examination* phase of Foucault's biopower, where they analyzed data to determine that Danny could not remain in general education settings for middle school. So he was pushed out of inclusion and into more segregated contexts.

While this type of medical model exclusion can occur with any child with disabilities, the intersecting oppressions of racism and ableism work in unique ways for children of color with disabilities, as their bodies are read as exceptionally deviant. Black children with disabilities, like Jeremiah, whose behaviors do not fit the rigid norms of school are seen as dangerous and unruly.[21] Dominant xenophobic narratives around immigration in US society make Latinx children with disabilities, like Sebastian, be seen as "other," deficient, and a burden.[22] And Asian children with disabilities, like Danny, are seen as exceptionally problematic and in need of controlling due to their deviation from the "model minority" myth.[23] Racism thus exacerbates the medical model tendency to restrict the bodies of children of color with disabilities. When they refuse to *enflesh* the docile-body norms of school, they are subjected to exclusion.

RESTRICTING THE LANGUAGE AND MEANING-MAKING OF CHILDREN OF COLOR WITH DISABILITIES

When I walk into Ms. Tejada's bilingual preschool classroom, I am surprised to see that the children are at work during center time because the room is so quiet. There are seventeen preschoolers sitting at various tables in designated centers: dramatic play, science, writing, reading, math, and art. Several of the centers are closed off, covered with large sheets of butcher paper with a sign attached to them reading, "Closed/Cerrado." The centers that are open are tidy, all of the materials organized into bins that are labeled in both English and Spanish. Each center has a sign hanging on a shelf that tells the children how many people are allowed in the center. The children are mostly working independently, although a few speak to each other in a quiet voice every now and then.

I walk over to the dramatic play area. There are three children seated at a round table in the middle of the center. At each child's seat is a paper mat that has shapes drawn onto them. Each shape is labeled with a different food or household item, such as milk, plate, spoon, and so on. I watch as the children take items from a basket placed in the center of the table and move them one by one to their designated spots on the mat. They then place the objects back in the basket and repeat this process over and over.

In my interview with Ms. Tejada following this observation, I asked her to share her views on center time and its purpose for young children. She said, "My classroom is very rigorous. Every moment is an opportunity to learn and prepare for life later on. You know nowadays Kindergarten is really first grade, so my kids have to be ready." Ms. Tejada went on to explain that because she had so many emergent bilinguals and children with IEPs in her classroom, it was especially important that they learn the "proper" ways of doing things so they could thrive in "very structured" kindergarten. "These kids come from families that don't know how to prepare them for the rigors of school in this country. It's my job to make sure they learn the language and are ready."

For Ms. Tejada, the need to make sure her children were "ready" for the future undergirded her dramatic play center. It was not, in her view, a place for children to engage in imaginary play. Rather, it was a center designed to help children learn functional behaviors and life skills. Ms. Tejada's deficit view of the children's families may have led her to being hyperfocused on correctness, as she tried to fill perceived gaps by teaching the children that there was only one way to interact with certain materials, or that table settings had to look one particular way. Ms. Tejada was enacting medical model–aligned interventions that served the aim of driving children toward a particular norm, where there was only one proper way to engage with and make sense of the world. The children's familial and community assets were not seen or valued; rather, their families were regarded as hindrances to thriving in school. As such, Ms. Tejada engaged in practices of erasure, attempting to replace the knowledge of the children's families with the knowledge of school.

When I mentioned to Ms. Tejada my surprise at how quiet the room was during center time, she shared, "I have a couple of children with IEPs who can get very loud and rowdy. So we've been practicing using our inside voices throughout the day." She also explained that the children with IEPs were the reason why several of the centers were closed: "I tried having blocks open from the beginning of the year, but it was too much for them. They couldn't build with them, just threw them around." Ms. Tejada restricted the language and meaning-making of all the children in the classroom because of behaviors that she observed in her children with disabilities that did not fit her expectations. In an effort to control how the children with IEPs used language and interacted with materials, Ms. Tejada enforced extreme limits so that the children would eventually learn to communicate and play in ways that felt correct to her.

Across my research in inclusion classrooms, I observed adults use medical model–aligned restrictions to force children of color with disabilities to adhere to the limited forms of linguistic expression and meaning-making that were accepted in the classroom. The primary goal with these restrictions was to teach children to internalize the "correct" ways of using language and making sense of the world around them. Sometimes such corrections manifested as preemptively providing strict guidelines for how children can communicate and interact. Other times, corrections were a reactive process of responding to children's language and meaning-making to steer them toward ways of thinking and communicating that were deemed appropriate.

I observed adults correcting children most frequently when the children of color with disabilities were also multilingual learners. The children were typically labeled as "English learners" and were part of families that had emigrated to the US from a different country. When the children read, wrote, or answered questions in ways that the adults deemed "incorrect," they would receive interventions. The grown-ups would use various strategies to push the child toward what they deemed to be the correct use of language. Here is an example from one observation in a second-grade Spanish-English dual immersion classroom:

> Ms. Dorian was working at a bean-shaped table with two children who had IEPs for specific learning disabilities, Jacinta and Lola. The class was engaged in independent writing in English. They had read a book called *The Important Book* and were writing paragraphs on nouns, describing what the most important thing about their selected nouns were. In a previous lesson, the students had created webs where they put the noun in the center and then had arms going out from the center with descriptions of the noun hanging from the outside.
>
> Jacinta chose to write her paragraph about umbrellas, and Lola chose to write her paragraph about dogs. Ms. Dorian had a laptop open to type the children's paragraphs for them. Ms. Dorian asked Jacinta to read her paragraph first. Jacinta had used inventive spelling in her paragraph and struggled to read some of her own writing. She paused frequently and hesitated as she read her sentence, "Theyr Is los of difrit yoos" (there is lots of different use). Ms. Dorian looked over Jacinta's shoulder and said, "Let's see here. Your paragraph makes sense, but there are a lot of words that are not spelled correctly." She took an eraser and began erasing words one by one. As she erased a word, she would prompt Jacinta to rewrite it, sounding out each letter of the word for her until Jacinta spelled it correctly.
>
> When they finished changing the spelling in Jacinta's paragraph, Ms. Dorian asked her to reread the paragraph to herself while she worked

with Lola on her paragraph. Lola had also used some inventive spelling in her paragraph about dogs, but she had an easier time making out her own writing. Her paragraph read, "The most important thing about dogs is that they're jere [hairy]. They are fure [furry]. They are fun. May [My] dog is a Jak Russl [Jack Russell]. But the most important thing about dogs is that they're fun." Ms. Dorian prompted Lola to read the paragraph to her as she typed. After Lola read the first sentence, Ms. Dorian paused her. "Is that really the most important thing about dogs?" Ms. Dorian asked Lola some additional questions about how dogs might help others, such as helping people who are unable to see with walking. After their discussion, Ms. Dorian gave Lola a new piece of paper, and Lola rewrote the paragraph so it began, "The most important thing about dogs is that they're helpful."

Jacinta and Lola experienced restriction of language through correction in two different ways. For Jacinta, her way of making out letter-sound relationships was corrected when Ms. Dorian erased her work and had her rewrite words that were not spelled in the standard way. The act of erasing Jacinta's written expression was a medical model–aligned practice, replacing Jacinta's undesirable language with normative, desirable language. So was Ms. Dorian's act of intervening on Lola's written ideas. The substance of Lola's paragraph did not match Ms. Dorian's ideas about what it means for something to be important (that it serves a useful purpose in society). She, therefore, prompted Lola to rewrite her paragraph. For both children, Ms. Dorian's actions communicated to them that their ways of using language and making sense of the world were wrong and therefore did not belong in the classroom.

Erasing the language and ideas of children of color with disabilities is a form of *linguicism,* where individuals experience discrimination and oppression based on their language.[24] Children of color with disabilities who are labeled as "English learners" often experience oppressive restrictions on their language because they are regarded as being particularly at risk for long-term school failure.[25] Rather than recognizing the linguistic richness of multilingual children with disabilities, educational practitioners frequently view this population from a deficit perspective, seeing them as having numerous obstacles to overcome to develop their academic English-language skills.[26]

The children's immigrant families are also viewed from a deficit perspective and framed as hindering the capacity of children with disabilities labeled as "English learners" to meet the norms of school.[27] For Ms. Dorian, her deficit view of families played a significant role in how she approached her work with her students labeled "English learners," especially those with disabilities. She was worried that the children's family backgrounds might make them particularly susceptible to experiencing academic delays. As she explained, "A lot of our [English learner] families are immigrants who you know have struggles, real struggles to get ahead. And so, their children therefore have these differences of experience, you know, that really ultimately do impact their school performance." She then went on to speak specifically about Jacinta's family:

> I find them to be irresponsible parents, and it's very frustrating. What I know is that they are not, they do not put school or learning as a priority. I think it is a huge disservice to their kids and highly irresponsible . . . I see that Jacinta is struggling just like all her siblings did, and she's often absent. I don't think she gets a lot of support, and I can't help but make a judgment on that. I'm not a parent, I don't have children, but I feel like, if you choose to bring children into this world, you need to be responsible and be involved in their growth and their learning. I think she tries as best she can, I don't see her as being fully engaged, though, which I think comes from this culture at home when parents care and are involved with the child at every stage of learning and encouraging them and telling them that learning is a priority. Then children will engage because they know that's the expectation both at home and at school. I just don't see that in her. She has a long way to go in terms of learning just the rules of grammar, spelling.

Because she saw Jacinta's family as not supporting their child's academic learning, Ms. Dorian felt that it was her responsibility to intervene and fill in the gaps that she perceived Jacinta as having. This deficit view of the family is what makes educators blind to the familial and community assets that children like Jacinta may bring with them to school. Not having the curiosity to learn more about what Jacinta is already doing with her language made it possible for Ms. Dorian to erase the language that Jacinta had worked hard to produce and replace it with language that Ms. Dorian regarded as correct—the language that Jacinta needed to be successful in school. Ms. Dorian's medical model–aligned approaches were, in her view, necessary to make up for the disadvantages that she felt Jacinta experienced due to the circumstances into which she was born.

In my research, children of color with disabilities who were labeled as "English learners" tended to be identified for language-related disabilities such as speech or language impairment, specific learning disabilities, and autism. Their IEP goals, therefore, often oriented educators toward practices that restricted the children's language and sensemaking. A Spanish-English bilingual third grader, Pamela, was one such child; she had an IEP for Speech or Language Impairment and Specific Learning Disabilities. Two of her IEP goals were as follows:

- Pamela will demonstrate competency in the use of grade-level sentences that are correct in form and content, during formal and informal therapies, in 4/5 opportunities.
- Pamela will be able to use a variety of reading strategies to decode and understand written information at her level, as measured by benchmark reading assessment to 80 percent accuracy, given specific intervention modeling and guided practice.

These goals were written in a way that pushed Pamela's educators toward a medical model interventionist approach. The focus was on ensuring that Pamela's language and literacy skills were "correct" and "accurate." Any language that fell outside these norms was problematic and did not belong in school. This emphasis on ensuring correctness was reflected in an observation of Pamela's one-on-one push-in session with her resource specialist teacher during an English literacy block:

> Mr. Richmond handed Pamela the book they were going to read together, *Pig's New House*. They started off with a book walk. Mr. Richmond had Pamela turn to page 4 and asked her what she noticed. She said, "That he's cutting wood," referring to the picture of the pig using a saw to cut pieces of wood. On page 5, Pamela said, "The sheeps is cutting wood too." On page 7, there was a picture of the animals working on Pig's house while he rested in a hammock and drank tea. Pamela said, "That's he's drinking some water?"
>
> Mr. Richmond asked Pamela, "Is he working?"
>
> Pamela said, "No."
>
> "Are other people working for him?" Mr. Richmond asked.
>
> "Yeah," Pamela said.
>
> Mr. Richmond then had Pamela turn to page 9. For this page, she said, "Now he's working, but the duck wants to help too." In the picture on this page, the pig was handing a duck a brick.
>
> Mr. Richmond responded, "Is he working, or are other people working for him?"
>
> Pamela said a bit hesitantly, "Other people?"
>
> "Are you noticing a pattern?" Mr. Richmond asked. Pamela shook her head no. "Are other people working for him?" Mr. Richmond tried. Pamela nodded. With this, Mr. Richmond asked Pamela to begin reading.
>
> Pamela read slowly and was frequently stopped to be corrected for her decoding. After a few errors, Mr. Richmond said to Pamela, "Remember to take your time when you're reading. You want to read every word on the page as it's written." After a few pages, Pamela began getting frustrated, sighing, and rolling her eyes as Mr. Richmond stopped her on every page, sometimes multiple times on one page.

When they got to the page where Pig was in the hammock, Mr. Richmond asked, "What do you notice?"

Pamela replied, "He's relaxing?"

"What is everyone else doing?" Mr. Richmond asked.

"Working?" Pamela answered with a question in her tone.

Mr. Richmond then said, "Whose house is this?" pointing to the house that was being built.

"Pig's," Pamela said.

When they finished the book, Mr. Richmond asked Pamela some comprehension questions. The first was, "Why did Pig build a new house?"

"Because he doesn't like his other house," Pamela replied. Mr. Richmond then had her turn back to the beginning of the book and asked her where Pig was living before. She said, "Because it was not like a house it was just like a outhouse." The picture was of Pig outdoors in the mud.

Mr. Richmond asked her, "What is he in?"

Pamela replied, "He's in like mud."

Then Mr. Richmond asked her, "What ended up happening?"

Pamela said, "First, they said they did it all."

Mr. Richmond stopped her, "You're going to the end. Even before that." He showed her the page where Pig was in the hammock again.

"That he just wants to relax cuz he just he was not doing nothing?" Pamela responded hesitantly.

Mr. Richmond asked her, "Was Pig doing any work?" She said, "No, just inviting their friends to like—" Pamela paused as if trying to think of a particular word.

In this one-on-one push-in intervention, we see that Mr. Richmond's focus on ensuring that Pamela decoded and comprehended the text correctly led to his frequently stopping her, asking her to reread words, and prompting her to answer his questions in a particular way. Mr. Richmond did not leave room for Pamela's linguistic expressions, which seemed to deviate from how he was reading and interpreting the text. This was true even when she showed signs of "understand[ing] written information," as her IEP goal states.

For instance, during the picture walk, Pamela communicated what she saw on each page; however, in an effort to preview the main idea of the text, Mr. Richmond redirected Pamela's focus to whether Pig was working. In their exchange after they had finished the book, Pamela told Mr. Richmond that Pig was building a house because "he doesn't like his other house . . . his outhouse." Dissatisfied with this interpretation of the text, Mr. Richmond directed Pamela through pointed questioning to get her to say that Pig was in the mud, even though to Pamela, she saw Pig's being in the mud as equivalent to his living in an "outhouse." At several points throughout their reading and conversation, Pamela responded to Mr. Richmond with a questioning tone, as if unsure whether she was giving the teacher the answers he sought. His regularly stopping and correcting Pamela also led to her showing signs of frustration. I later overheard Pamela say to a friend, "He talks too much and doesn't listen."

Corrective moves that serve to restrict the linguistic expression and sensemaking of children of color with disabilities may be well intended, aimed at helping children achieve success in a school system that narrowly accepts only one way of speaking, reading, writing, and thinking. However, they are interventions that erase the languages, understandings, and ideas that children bring with them to school. Multilingual children of color with disabilities have tremendous assets that often go ignored in schools because of the medical model–driven urgency around pushing children toward a particular norm—one that prioritizes standard academic English.[28] It is the adults' failure to listen with an ear to understand rather than to change that makes correction the default interaction between teacher and student. As such, multilingual children of color with disabilities' ways of using language and sensemaking are excluded from the classroom.

Correction of language and meaning-making does not always involve verbal language. In my observations in inclusion classrooms, children also expressed themselves through the use of materials. The children of color with disabilities whom I observed frequently interacted with materials to express their sensemaking in ways that were not deemed appropriate by the adults working with them. For example, I once observed in a third-grade inclusion classroom as students were working on creating posters to present the information that they gathered on their research projects for Earth Day. For their research, the children all selected various topics related to the environment. Jimena, a child with an IEP for Speech or Language Impairments and Autism, chose to do her research on the rainforest. She was working with her paraprofessional on coloring in cutouts of animal drawings to add to her poster. As Jimena was coloring her animal cutouts, her teacher, Ms. Valdes, came over and said, "Oh no, a jaguar is not black. Let's try again." Ms. Valdes looked through the stack of animal drawings on the table and pulled out another picture of a jaguar. Ms. Valdes turned to Jimena's paraprofessional and said, "This should be tan with black and orange spots, not black all over. Also, help her to stay in the lines. Sometimes if you do hand over hand, it can help her with coloring in the lines." Although Jimena's interpretation of the jaguar led her to color it in black, Ms. Valdes felt that it was important to correct Jimena and ensure that she used the proper colors. In this way, she reactively limited Jimena's expression and meaning-making. How Jimena saw and made sense of jaguars was seen as not valuable, as it led her astray from the "correct" way that jaguars should look in Ms. Valdes's view.

In a different classroom, I observed as the first-grade children were working on solving math problems with Unifix cubes. The children were told to pull out their plastic bins that held their individual cubes. Andre, a Black Haitian child with an IEP for Other Health Impairment (ADHD), took out his bin full of black and white Unifix cubes. The teachers instructed the children to organize their cubes into groups of three. Andre created stacks of three Unifix cubes and then arranged them so that they looked like a piano keyboard. One teacher walked over to Andre's table, saw what he had done, and said, "Fix your cubes. You know you're not supposed to be doing that right now." Andre then reorganized his Unifix cube stacks so they were lined up in rows of black and rows of white.

This example with Andre and the Unifix cubes shows how the medical model can make educators blind to the creativity, knowledge, and assets of children of color with disabilities. The teacher's rigid idea about how the children should be working with the Unifix cubes limited her ability to see that Andre had indeed done what he was told to do—organize the cubes into groups of three. Andre had just seen in those groupings a creative way to display his cubes, as he made an out-of-the-box association with something else in the world that he had previously experienced. Andre was demonstrating complex, abstract thinking, but this was not recognized because he did not follow the normative script for how to work with the Unifix cubes as the teachers had instructed. Andre experienced this type of correction with some regularity. He eventually disengaged as the year progressed, refusing to participate in work and often being sent to the principal's office.

All the examples in this chapter show how the medical model of disability works with racism and linguicism to try and force children of color with disabilities to conform to particular norms. Such conformity is a form of erasure. Children's many assets are ignored, and their existing ways of being are perceived as deficits. It is important to note that the educators described in this chapter are not to be blamed on an individual level. All were engaging in practices that they felt were necessary to help their children of color with disabilities to thrive in school. What is at issue, therefore, is not individual teachers, but an educational system that is designed to privilege some ways of being and erase others. When children are pushed to change how they move, communicate, and make meaning, this does not always lead to the assimilation desired. In fact, it can lead to confusion and sometimes resistance on the part of the child. As children of color with disabilities are subjected to medical model–aligned interventions, they become further othered in their inclusion classrooms, which can ultimately lead to their exclusion.

Medical model–aligned practices, therefore, do little to support the inclusion of children of color with disabilities. Rather, the more children are expected to change, the more likely they are to be seen as problems needing to be fixed. Such perspectives do not cultivate a culture of belonging. So long as the medical model continues to be the dominant model in inclusion classrooms, children of color with disabilities will experience exclusion along many dimensions. If we want inclusion classrooms to be places where all children truly belong, then we must move away from practices that align with a normative medical model. Instead, we must engage in humanizing approaches that aim to honor children of color with disabilities rather than change them. In the rest of this book, I aim to show, with concrete, specific examples, how educators can refuse the medical model of disability and embrace a more humanizing pedagogy of belonging with their children of color with disabilities.

2

Refusing the Medical Model Using a Discrit Lens

THE (RE)IMAGINING THAT I propose in this book is grounded in the principles of Disability Critical Race Studies (DisCrit). Bringing together ideas and arguments from disability studies in education and critical race theory, Annamma, Connor, and Ferri (2013) developed DisCrit to address a critical gap that they identified in our knowledge base. Disability studies scholars were often ignoring issues of race, while critical race theory scholars did not attend to disability, despite the reality that racism and ableism are inextricably linked in schools and society. DisCrit focuses on how race and disability are socially co-constructed in complex ways that systemically oppress children of color with disabilities. Children of color with disabilities are positioned uniquely in schools because, as Annamma and colleagues explain, "Racism and ableism are normalizing processes that are interconnected and collusive. In other words, racism and ableism often work in ways that are unspoken, yet racism validates and reinforces ableism, and ableism validates and reinforces racism."[1]

DisCrit scholarship centers on the experiences of children of color with disabilities, interrogating how macro-level, systemic racism and ableism are enacted in the daily lives of the children, their families, and their teachers. Such an examination involves looking at how racism and ableism work interdependently to uphold notions of normalcy, as well as at how individuals and groups engage in activism and resistance against these normalizing forces. These goals of DisCrit are central to this book. I am particularly interested in how educators refuse deficit-oriented, medical model-aligned, normalizing perspectives that cause harm in the lives of children of color with disabilities. The educators I have met who practice these acts of refusal are creating DisCrit Classroom Ecologies daily. Annamma and Morrison's (2018) framework for a DisCrit Classroom Ecology is a response to the dysfunctional ecologies in classrooms and schools where multiply marginalized children of color are not positioned as valuable resources. In dysfunctional ecologies, which are driven by the medical model of disability, children of color with disabilities are seen as deficient and are acted upon with harmful practices, such as the pathologizing, exclusionary approaches described in chapter 1. The concept of a DisCrit Classroom Ecology counteracts these narratives by drawing on W. E. B. DuBois's gift theory, where children of color are seen as possessing extraordinary gifts due to their experiences with oppression.[2]

A DisCrit Classroom Ecology is comprised of three constructs. The first is DisCrit Curriculum, which involves students' learning about their own identities and histories, as well as about structural injustice. The second is DisCrit Pedagogy, where educators learn about and teach to students' many wide-ranging gifts. The third is DisCrit Solidarity, which is when teachers view students' actions as Strategies of Resistance and work with the children to channel that resistance in ways that dismantle injustice. Running through all three constructs is DisCrit Resistance. When educators aim to establish DisCrit Classroom Ecologies, they are engaging in DisCrit Resistance. Educators reject deficit-based views of multiply marginalized students of color with disabilities and instead see their capabilities. Behaviors that are often deemed problematic in the status quo of schooling are reframed as gifts to be welcomed because educators enacting DisCrit Resistance recognize how the children are repositioning themselves to fight power, authority, and oppression. The educator thus resists the status quo alongside each student, seeking ways to dismantle inequity and find opportunities for the child to be seen, valued, known, and therefore able to thrive.[3] This is a form of activism that Annamma and colleagues call for in their theory of DisCrit. The seventh tenet of DisCrit states, "DisCrit requires activism and supports all forms of resistance."[4]

Reconceptualizing an entire classroom ecology involves examining the relationships between all people and systems. Ecology is, after all, the study of how organisms relate to each other and to their physical surroundings. I, however, focus specifically on the relationship between teachers and children of color with disabilities, as these relationships often determine whether a child will experience belonging or exclusion in school. As Annamma and Morrison explain, educators are powerful parts of students' learning ecologies because their actions can reinforce or dislocate systemic intersecting oppressions. I also look primarily at DisCrit Pedagogy and DisCrit Solidarity. Because exclusionary practices often occur as a result of practitioners' perceptions of and actions toward children of color with disabilities, I am particularly interested in how educators reframe and reposition children who are seen as problems in classrooms. If we consider the examples of medical model–aligned practice described in the previous chapter, we see how educators' views of and responses to children were driving forces in the children's experiences with exclusion. Teachers enacted narrow pedagogies that matched their limited view of what counts as acceptable ways of being and thinking, which then led them to see children of color with disabilities as problems that needed to be fixed. The result was interventionist approaches with the aim of changing the children rather than welcoming and cultivating their gifts.

As pedagogy, interactions, and relationships are drivers of the medical model's pervasiveness, DisCrit Pedagogy and DisCrit Solidarity are critical constructs that stand in stark contrast to the status quo practices that lead to exclusion. But what are the pedagogical moves that educators make to build on and enhance children's gifts, and how do educators respond to children's Strategies of Resistance in ways that refuse medical model–aligned oppressive practices and cultivate environments of belonging? While the DisCrit Classroom Ecology framework is explained conceptually, what it looks like in practice is less well defined. The chapters that follow aim to address this gap in our knowledge base by offering a concrete depiction of DisCrit Pedagogy and DisCrit Solidarity in action. The purpose of the examples given in this book is to show what is possible when educators commit to resisting systemic oppression of their students of color with disabilities and value the children as important assets in their classrooms.

A CLOSER LOOK AT DISCRIT PEDAGOGY

If medical model–aligned practices are characterized by narrow, normalizing definitions of appropriate ways of being, then a DisCrit Pedagogy is characterized by its expansiveness. The teacher sees children's many assets and builds on them to create expansive learning environments. Behaviors often seen as deficits are reconceptualized as gifts to be harnessed. For example, a child's nonstandard responses to reading comprehension questions are not viewed as wrong and indicative of deficiencies in literacy development; instead, the teacher asks questions with the aim of genuinely seeking to understand the child's thinking because the child's ideas are important and valuable. To harness the many gifts of children of color with disabilities requires providing them with multiple entry points and modalities for engaging with learning.[5]

Hancock and colleagues (2021) draw from the principles of Universal Design for Learning (UDL) in their definition of DisCrit Pedagogy. As the authors write, "Educators can draw on asset-based pedagogies to implement multiple and varied representations of content, opportunities for children's engagement, and expressions of child learning (Center for Applied Special Technology, 2011) with consideration of the interconnected nature of racism and ableism (Waitoller & Thorius, 2016)."[6] Multiple means of engagement, means of representation, and means of action and expression are incorporated into the inclusion classroom to ensure that all children have access to instruction.

In the UDL framework, engagement is the *why* of learning. Providing multiple means of engagement means finding many ways to stimulate children's interest and motivation in learning. Representation is the *what* of learning. Offering multiple means of representation involves presenting information and content in a variety of ways. Action and expression constitute the *how* of learning. Providing multiple means of action and expression involves giving children many options for expressing what they know.[7] In a universally designed classroom, the emphasis on accessibility ensures that all children are part of the learning process. Children are not positioned as deficient when their learning styles do not align with the teaching styles of the classroom. Educators are to change the environment to fit the child, not change the child to fit the environment.

Embracing a DisCrit Pedagogy thus requires reorganizing the power dynamics and structures of an inclusion classroom so children are centered as important agents of knowledge production. In a DisCrit Classroom Ecology, children have the power to make choices about how to engage in and share their learning. The educators create an environment that enables children to make these choices, but they follow the lead of the children without dictating how they should learn or what counts as valuable learning. In DisCrit Pedagogy, therefore, educators are co-constructors alongside children, building upon their strengths to generate learning opportunities that give children the opportunity to create knowledge and take ownership of the learning process.

A CLOSER LOOK AT DISCRIT SOLIDARITY

DisCrit Solidarity is a direct response to the "hypersurveillance, hyperlabeling, and hyperpunishment, that animates the discourse, policies, and practices of managing students and classrooms."[8] Narrow definitions of appropriate behavior in medical model–aligned inclusion classrooms often lead to surveillance and restriction—precursors to ultimate exclusion. Annamma and Morrison (2018) explain that children of color with disabilities are particularly subjected to restrictive pedagogies of pathologization because their ways of being often do not fit the norms of school. Rejecting the continued focus on classroom or behavior management, therefore, is a critical aspect of DisCrit Solidarity. Teachers who practice DisCrit Solidarity understand that the education system is oppressive to children who do not conform to the norm. They see behaviors that are typically viewed as disruptive or problems to be fixed as Strategies of Resistance—creative and brilliant ways that children refuse conformity and oppression. Strategies of Resistance are tools of survival for children of color with disabilities who are confronted with erasure.[9] Teachers who practice DisCrit Solidarity recognize the range of emotions that children of color with disabilities bring with them in response to the structural and interpersonal violence that they experience in schools. They aim to channel these emotions to dismantle systemic inequities rather than solely trying to control children and prevent them from expressing their emotions.[10]

DisCrit Solidarity thus requires seeing children of color with disabilities in radically different ways. Children who are crying, hitting, and throwing things are not labeled as a problem; rather, they are seen as children communicating an experience of pain—something wrong in the environment that needs to change. It is the focus on the environment, not the child, that serves as the critical starting point for a teacher enacting DisCrit Solidarity. Educators move away from trying to manage or control the children and instead aim to change the environment. This does not mean that behavior changes are not needed or desired.

Teachers who practice DisCrit Solidarity work to shift the environment so the children feel known, valued, and cared for, such that they do not need to practice Strategies of Resistance. As Annamma and Handy (2019) put it, the classroom becomes "a sanctuary to identify, display and address emotions and behaviours, and concomitantly channel that passion to change the system."[11]

The goal in DisCrit Solidarity, then, is to create a classroom community grounded in authentic relationships, healing, and an ethic of care.[12] Migliarini and Annamma (2019) say about DisCrit Solidarity:

> Educators must seek to build relationships with multiply marginalized students of color rooted not in obedience but in solidarity and expansive notions of justice. We draw from Mohanty (2003) who defines solidarity "in terms of mutuality, accountability, and the recognition of common interests as the basis for relationships" (p. 7). Each of these things must be present in educators' pedagogical philosophy—a belief in reciprocal relationships wherein students are partners, a commitment to responsibility for the outcomes students experience, and shared goals with students that are explicitly articulated.[13]

As relationships and care are essential to DisCrit Solidarity, there is an understanding that if one child is hurting, the whole community is hurting. Changes must be made to support every child and thus facilitate well-being for the entire community.[14] Teachers who practice DisCrit Solidarity prioritize healing and healthy relationships for their children of color with disabilities who are hurting. They know that to have an authentic, caring community requires that all members feel well and whole.

DISCRIT-ALIGNED TEACHERS

While there is much theoretical literature on DisCrit and a DisCrit Classroom Ecology, less has been written on what these concepts look like in practice. For us to be able to (re)imagine inclusion for children of color with disabilities, we need to be able to visualize what genuine inclusive practice might entail. After observing in many medical model–aligned classrooms where exclusion of children of color with disabilities was the norm, I became tired of consistently spending time in settings where children of color with disabilities were dehumanized. I knew from my experience of that sole inclusion classroom described in the introduction of this book that a different vision of schooling for children of color with disabilities was possible. I decided to pursue research projects that focused on educators engaging in radical, child-centered, and humanizing practices. I joined the Agency for Young Children Research Collective, led by Dr. Jennifer Keys Adair at the University of Texas at Austin, which engages in community-based partnerships with schools and classrooms that are committed to enhancing agency for young children of color. I also launched my own projects aimed at documenting the approaches of educators who foster true inclusion for children of color with disabilities.

After years of conducting participant-observation research, I realized that I had collected enough data from my various projects to operationalize the pedagogical and relational moves that teachers make to create a DisCrit Classroom Ecology for their children of color with disabilities. I revisited the data with the aim of analyzing how DisCrit-aligned teachers enact Annamma and Morrison's framework to offer practitioners, teacher educators, and policy makers a more concrete picture of what it takes to ensure that children of color with disabilities experience belonging in school.

The schools and programs included in my dataset are settings where significant numbers of children of color with disabilities spend 80 percent or more of their school day in the general education classroom, learning alongside their nondisabled peers. This percentage is what the US Department of Education uses as an indicator of the highest level of inclusion. All the schools and programs are ones where at least 50 percent of the enrollment is children of color with a range of racial backgrounds. Typically, I observed in classrooms that the school leaders recommended I visit because the teachers enacted practices that they deemed particularly strong for fostering belonging and child-centered learning. In smaller programs, I was able to observe in all the classrooms.

While reanalyzing my data, I used the DisCrit Classroom Ecology framework as a guide to identify those teachers who offered evidence of alignment with DisCrit Pedagogy and DisCrit Solidarity. Educators who appeared to have strong relationships with their students of color with disabilities, who followed the children's lead, who gave them choices for how they engaged with instruction and showed their meaning-making—these were the educators I identified as enacting a DisCrit Classroom Ecology, and whom I included in my analysis for this book. One of the strongest signs of a DisCrit-aligned classroom was the joy that I sensed in the children. These were classrooms where children showed affection and care toward each other and toward their teachers; where they eagerly, and with broad smiles, jumped in to help their teachers and each other; and where the children's enthusiasm for the activities they engaged in was palpable, with energy running through their bodies and ringing in their voices. These classrooms were the ones I sought to learn more about.

In total, my DisCrit-aligned participants included thirty-five teachers in twenty-one classrooms. Although I was not specifically looking for teachers of color, the majority did turn out to be of color. Of the thirty-five teachers, only four were white; the remaining were Latinx, Black, multiracial, or Asian. Eight of the classrooms were integrated co-teaching settings in which there was one general education head teacher and one special education head teacher. Three classrooms each had one head teacher and two assistants. The head teachers in the classrooms all had at least five years of teaching experience, with most having eight to twelve years of experience. The most experienced teacher had thirty years of teaching experience. All but two teachers identified as female. Twenty of the teachers were certified in special and general education, while fifteen were certified in just general education. The teachers taught in grades preK through fifth grade.

My data collection involved qualitative, participant observation methods.[15] Depending on the teachers' availability, I observed in their classrooms for one to three full school days. With permission from the students' families, I held preparatory conversations with each teacher, during which they gave me background information on the children of color with individualized education programs (IEPs) in the room. As I observed in the classrooms, I specifically paid attention to the interactions between the teachers and their children of color with disabilities. I wrote jottings that later became detailed, descriptive field notes, focused on the ways that teachers organized learning for children of color with disabilities, as well as how they related to the children in terms of their language, tone, and physical movements.[16] In my field notes, I aimed to include as many details from the days of observation as I could, describing each moment as a scene from a particular day to portray a vivid picture of each teacher's work in the classroom.

In my analysis, I organized the various scenes under the categories of DisCrit Pedagogy and DisCrit Solidarity, finding examples that show what each construct looks like in practice. I coded the examples using an inductive, grounded theory, open coding–axial coding–selective coding process.[17] From the coding emerged several themes for each DisCrit construct. For DisCrit Pedagogy, I found the following themes: *Responding with Respect not Restriction, Making Room for the Unexpected,* and *Centering Inquiry.* For DisCrit Solidarity, I found the following themes: *Recognizing the Gifts of Resistance* and *Centering Relationships.* I wrote thematic narratives for each theme, which serve as the bases for the chapters that follow.[18]

In addition to the field notes, I interviewed every classroom's teacher/teaching team twice. The interviews each lasted about an hour. They were semistructured and included questions about the educators' backgrounds, teaching philosophies, beliefs about children with disabilities, and thoughts on inclusion. I also asked the teachers about specific practices that I observed in their classrooms. I described moments that I observed that stood out to me and asked the teachers to reflect on those moments, sharing what was going on for them and why they made the moves they made. All the interviews were audio-recorded and transcribed, and the transcripts were used in the writing of the thematic narratives. I incorporated specific quotes from teachers whose practices I described under each theme to give more depth and rationale to each move that the educators made.

The examples I share in the chapters that follow showcase teachers who daily commit to cultivating communities of belonging for their children of color with disabilities. This very commitment is at the heart of a DisCrit Classroom Ecology. What flows from this commitment are pedagogical and interpersonal moves that make it possible for children of color with disabilities to not only be included in classrooms with their nondisabled peers, but also to thrive. To be clear, the teachers whose practices are described in this book were not educators who never engaged in medical model–aligned approaches. The pervasiveness of the medical model means that even the teacher who wholeheartedly embraces DisCrit Resistance can enact normalizing pathologization in an inclusion classroom. The teachers in this book, however, do adhere to the concepts of DisCrit Pedagogy and DisCrit Solidarity in ways that eliminate exclusion from the experiences of children of color with disabilities. It was not the amount of time spent with nondisabled peers that ultimately made these classrooms inclusive. The inclusion classrooms were characterized by how every child was viewed and positioned as a valuable, resourceful, and important member of the community.

Although I am humbled and awestruck by all the teachers I write about in this book, my focus is actually not on the individual educators. My focus is on the specific decisions and moves they make in response to the children in their care. I spotlight practices rather than individuals in order to emphasize that any educator is capable of creating a DisCrit

Classroom Ecology. By zooming in on and codifying specific pedagogical and interpersonal moves, I aim to show that it is possible for inclusion to be (re)imagined for *all* children of color with disabilities. In fact, often the shifts that need to be made for children of color with disabilities to experience belonging are not that large, but they are nonetheless significant and radical. My hope is to demonstrate how small, moment-by-moment decisions can make a very big difference in the experiences of children of color with disabilities. All teachers can make this difference, so long as they believe that children of color with disabilities are valuable members of their classroom communities.

II

(Re)Imagining Toward DisCrit Pedagogy in Inclusion Classrooms

3

Responding with Respect Not Restriction

I REMEMBER GROWING UP in Jamaica always feeling like I had two selves: my school self, who followed rules and was really quiet, and my self at home, who could be a bit more free. I was really shy and timid at school, but I wasn't actually like that at home. I want my students to feel like they can be their true selves all the time, not just at home, but at school too. — Ms. Allen, kindergarten inclusion teacher

Honoring children's "true selves" is a hallmark trait of all the inclusion classrooms that I observed where DisCrit Pedagogy was present. Classroom teachers, like Ms. Allen, refused narrow ideas about what counts as *appropriate* ways of being. Rather than labeling and stigmatizing the behavior of their students of color with disabilities, the educators reframed the children's behavior as strengths to build upon. The priority was creating environments where children could be their full selves and respected as such.

I observed this type of respect show up in Ms. Allen's classroom acutely in her work with a child I'll call Mario. Mario was a five-year-old child with an individualized education program (IEP) for Autism and Speech or Language Impairment. He had recently immigrated to the US from Central America and predominantly spoke Spanish. Ms. Allen's classroom was not bilingual, and neither she nor her assistant teacher, Ms. Campbell, spoke Spanish fluently. Their class included many Spanish speakers, however, and the teachers welcomed the use of children's home languages in their classroom. When Mario communicated verbally, he used mostly Spanish, while also mixing in some English. Much of his communication, however, was through his body. Mario frequently moved through the classroom at a quick pace, with his arms extended out to his sides as if he were trying to catch the wind with his whole body. He communicated interest by going directly over to whatever caught his eye and touching it with his hands. He communicated lack of interest by pushing things or people away from him, sometimes with an accompanying vocalization that sounded like a shriek or a yelp.

Mario often participated in academic experiences using modes of expression that differed from the dominant uses of language present in the classroom. I observed an example of this during a writing lesson. The class was in the midst of a unit on poetry. Ms. Allen had just led the class in a review of different features of poems before sending them off to work on their own poems:

> The children sprang to their feet and walked over to their table areas, where they pulled out red folders from the organizers hanging on the backs of their chairs. One child walked around the room carrying a bucket of pencils and passed them out to her peers. Other children walked over to a set of shelves in the middle of the room and pulled out paper for their writing. There was an enthusiastic buzz in the room as children chatted with each other about their work, read their poems to one another, and shared coloring materials.

> Mario sat at a table nestled by the block area with three other peers. He pulled out two pieces of paper from his writing folder. He crumpled one up in his hands, turning it into what looked like a bow tie. He then took a pencil and began to poke holes in his paper. A peer looked over at Mario and said, "That's a cool poem," then turned back to his own writing. Mario then took the second piece of paper and began ripping it into small pieces. He worked on fitting the little pieces into the holes he poked on his bow-tie paper. Ms. Allen came over to Mario, knelt down beside him, and said, "Tell me about your work." Mario held up his paper creation and said "Mariposa!" He pointed to the poem on the Smartboard at the front of the room. The class had earlier read a poem on butterflies, which tied to the larger butterfly study they were engaging in.
>
> Ms. Allen then asked Mario what he wanted to say about butterflies. She asked a peer to help translate when Mario said words in Spanish that she did not know. Ms. Allen wrote Mario's ideas on a piece of paper: "Mariposa is small. It has spots. It flies. Mariposa."

In this scene, Ms. Allen embraced Mario's expression of his ideas through his paper creation of the butterfly. She allowed for an expansive interpretation of writing poetry, rather than restricting Mario to fit into a standard definition of poetry writing. What struck me the most when I observed this scene play out was that Ms. Allen did not approach Mario with the assumption that he was off-task. I, myself, had made the assumption that Mario was not engaging in poetry writing but was instead working on a creative, sensory task that had nothing to do with poetry at all. I think that many adults may have thought similarly about Mario's behavior. Ms. Allen, however, entered her interaction with Mario with an open mind. She neither assumed that he was working on poetry nor that he was not. She simply knelt beside him and said, "Tell me about your work," giving Mario the space to share without imposing an interpretation or expectation onto him. In this way, Ms. Allen respected Mario's true self.

We see how this respect for children's many ways of being was transferred to the other children in the classroom as well. When Mario's peer turned over to him and said, "That's a cool poem," the peer was also demonstrating an expansiveness toward work in the classroom. The child saw Mario's work as potentially being an alternative means of expressing his poetic ideas. This child's behavior indicated to me that Ms. Allen and her assistant had created an environment where children's many modes of expression were welcomed and accepted. In this way, they had cultivated a classroom of belonging for all children.

Ms. Allen's embrace of children's different ways of being—her honoring of children's true selves—reflected her beliefs about child development. She said in her interview that a big worry that she had about early childhood was that many educators do "not realize that children are living human beings too, and that they're all different. They all have their own emotions, and they have their own opinions. And I see it all the time. It's like the expectation is for children to just be little robots, and to do what you tell them to do, you know?" Ms. Allen's desire to enact a more humanizing pedagogy with her children led her to interact with the children of color with IEPs in her room with a genuine curiosity. In her quest to honor her students' "true selves," she saw all expression as a form of communication—a way for the grown-ups to get a glimpse into the children and then follow their lead on how to engage with their learning. Ms. Allen actively did not want her children to be "little robots" who conformed to external expectations. She wanted the children to be able to be their own individual selves in her classroom.

One way that Ms. Allen communicated to the children that their ways of being were accepted in the classroom was by trusting them. When children got up out of their seats, when they spoke to each other during independent work time or lessons, or when they moved their bodies in unexpected ways (such as when one child suddenly shot up in the air during circle time to stretch his body), Ms. Allen did not reprimand them. She assumed good intent. Ms. Allen believed that her children "owned the room. The classroom is theirs." She was not interested in restricting the children because she trusted them to do whatever they needed to do to engage in the learning.

In fact, that is precisely what I observed them doing: moving and behaving in ways that supported their interactions with learning materials and processes. For example, children often got up and walked around the room to use resources hanging in the classroom, such as word walls, number charts, and labels in their choice time centers. They also went to retrieve materials that they needed for their work, such as scissors, pencils, or staplers. Sometimes children moved around to get a tissue for themselves or to clean their hands with sanitizer. Other times, they got up to move simply for the sake of moving, because that is what their bodies were telling them they needed (such as when a child stood up from his chair to jump a few times and then sat right back down). By not reprimanding the children, Ms. Allen and Ms. Campbell reinforced the norm that children were to be trusted to do what they needed in order to learn. When children asked for permission to move their bodies or direct their own learning, the teachers reminded them that they were trusted. I observed a child ask Ms. Allen one day if he could get the stapler for his book-making work, and she responded, "You don't need to ask, papa. You know what to do." The child smiled and immediately got up from his seat to retrieve the stapler from a classroom shelf.

One might think that a classroom where children were able to move as they pleased and were not expected to always be still and quiet would be a chaotic environment. Ms. Allen and Ms. Campbell's room, however, always felt orderly. There was a low buzz in the room throughout the day, but it was joyful and engaged. The children were constantly busy and at work; their movement and talk were intentional. The trust that was communicated to them by their teachers seemed to motivate them to truly take ownership of their learning and remain engaged. The fact that all children were respected and trusted meant that the children of color with IEPs in the room were not made to feel *other*. They were not stigmatized for their ways of being. They were given the freedom to move, learn, and interact as they needed. Because respect for all was the norm, the children with IEPs experienced the same kind of belonging and acceptance as their nondisabled peers did.

Having observed in many kindergarten classrooms where children were expected to sit still and be quiet, Ms. Allen's philosophy of letting children move as they saw fit struck me as countercultural, a direct contrast to the culture of schooling described in the introduction of this book. Ms. Allen's goal of honoring children's true selves made her interact with her children in ways that aligned with the aspect of DisCrit Pedagogy where teachers "(re)organize learning to shift power in the classroom."[1] By working with children in ways that made it possible for them to have a voice in how they wanted to learn, Ms. Allen engaged in power sharing with her children.

This power sharing is what made it possible for Justin, a child with attention deficit hyperactivity disorder (ADHD) and suspected learning disabilities, to tell his teachers, "I need a break" during a writing lesson. He then became Ms. Campbell's helper, following her around the room as she met with other children in the classroom and handing her supplies as she needed them. Power sharing is also what made it possible for Monica, a Spanish-dominant speaker with an IEP for Speech or Language Impairment, to ask one of her peers for help during a phonics lesson. Her peer and Monica shared a phonics board and worked together to follow the teacher's instructions. It was power sharing that also gave Alyssa, a child with an IEP for Speech or Language Impairment and Specific Learning Disabilities, the freedom to show her thinking during a math lesson by using all drawings and no numbers. Ms. Allen later talked with Alyssa about her thinking, and they used Unifix cubes to create math sentences based on Alyssa's drawings.

In addition to this redistribution of power that facilitated a climate of *respect and not restriction*, Ms. Allen and Ms. Campbell demonstrated respect for the children through affection. Both teachers communicated with the children using warm, loving tones. They laughed with the children, asked them about their home lives, and apologized when the children called out their mistakes. Both also often used "love," "mama," "papa," and "my dear" when speaking to individual children. Children came up to the teachers to give them hugs randomly throughout the day, as if just wanting to get a burst of tender loving care before continuing with their work. When children showed feelings of sadness or anger, the teachers spoke to them with genuine concern, wanting to know why the children felt as they did and what could help them feel better. Ms. Campbell said about the teachers' affection toward the children, "You have to love them. They know. The children know if you love them, and they know when you don't. This don't work if you don't love them." What I heard in Ms. Campbell's comment was an understanding that children needed to feel that they were genuinely loved—as they are—for the classroom to be a community of belonging, where everyone learns.

The love that the teachers had for the children trickled down into love that the children showed one another. Just as they spontaneously hugged their teachers, the children also hugged one another throughout the day. They were very quick to help one another. Cleanup after choice time was remarkably fast, as children called out "I can help!" to their peers and assisted each other with putting things away. They were just as quick to comfort a peer in distress. During one of my observations, a new child joined the classroom community. Ms. Allen greeted the child, gave her a tour of the room, and introduced her to the class during morning meeting. When she asked for a volunteer to be the new student's buddy, all the children's hands shot up in the air. Throughout the day, the children declared to every adult they saw in the hallway or in specials classes, "We have a new student in our class!" before introducing the child to whoever would listen.

There was one child in the class, Jamar, who had an IEP for Autism. Jamar frequently reacted to changes in routine with tears and shouting. One day, he stood up from the rug, ready to do his job of changing the daily schedule. He quickly realized, though, that someone else had already done his job. Jamar collapsed to the ground and began to cry while kicking his legs. Ms. Allen came over and crouched down next to Jamar. Several children stood up and surrounded Ms. Allen and Jamar. After a few seconds of letting Jamar get his tears and emotions out, Ms. Allen helped Jamar to his feet and walked him over to a chair by the rug. She encouraged him to take a few deep breaths. Two of Jamar's peers stood behind Jamar and began patting his back, saying, "It's OK. You can do it tomorrow."

This example with Jamar shows the strong culture of acceptance and care that was established in Ms. Allen's kindergarten classroom. While I do believe that children have a proclivity for creating truly inclusive communities, I also know that they are affected by the behaviors and attitudes of the adults around them. Ms. Allen and Ms. Campbell modeled what it means to respect all children and cultivate a community of belonging, which allowed the children to tap into their proclivity for inclusion.

THE PRACTICES OF *RESPONDING WITH RESPECT NOT RESTRICTION*

There are so many practices at play in Ms. Allen's kindergarten inclusion classroom that align with DisCrit Pedagogy. I'll call out three that Ms. Allen and Ms. Campbell enact to promote *respect not restriction*. The first practice is *welcoming all forms of engaging with learning and presenting ideas*. We see this in how Ms. Allen interacted with Mario about his poetry writing, as well as in Ms. Allen's expansive stance toward children's movement and behavior in the classroom. The second practice is *expecting and trusting children to take ownership of their learning*. Both Ms. Allen and Ms. Campbell were able to respect children's wide range of movements and behaviors because they trusted the children to do what they needed to do to learn. The teachers did not jump to the conclusion that children were misbehaving. Instead, they assumed that children were taking control of their learning processes. When they saw unexpected behaviors, they started with curiosity, approaching the children with a desire to understand rather than to reprimand. Finally, Ms. Allen and Ms. Campbell showed *genuine affection, love, and care* toward the children, which facilitated an entire classroom community of respect. By loving the children as they are, they inspired them to also practice love and acceptance of one another. There was, therefore, no need to restrict children's behaviors because of the collective respect for all ways of being that the entire community showed and experienced.

Through these practices, the children in Ms. Allen's kindergarten classroom were honored for their "true selves." Next, I offer three additional examples, one for each of the practices described here that facilitated a DisCrit Pedagogy of *respect not restriction* for children of color with disabilities in inclusion classrooms.

WELCOMING ALL FORMS OF ENGAGEMENT WITH LEARNING

In their DisCrit framework for early childhood teacher education, Hancock and colleagues (2021) draw on the principles of Universal Design for Learning (UDL) to argue that varied and multiple means of representation, action and expression, and engagement counteract the deficit perspectives often held about children of color with disabilities.[2] This approach to designing "expansive learning opportunities" for children of color with disabilities is a way that DisCrit-aligned educators "disrupt *status quo* perceptions and explore the multidimensional assets that multiply-marginalized Students of Color bring."[3] While in Ms. Allen's classroom, *respect not restriction* was often a responsive practice where educators responded to children's varied forms of expression with love and validation, in other classrooms, *respect not restriction* was enacted more structurally through the organization of the learning environment.

This was the case in Ms. Shima and Ms. Davis's second-grade classroom. When I visited their classroom community, Ms. Shima and Ms. Davis were the head teachers in an integrated, co-teaching classroom. Ms. Shima was the general education teacher and Ms. Davis was the special education teacher; however, an outsider walking into the classroom would not be able to recognize these distinctions, as the two shared full responsibility for implementing instruction and supporting all their learners on an individual and collective basis. There were twenty-one children in their classroom, six of whom had IEPs and two who were being considered for special education services. The class was over 50 percent children of color who identified as Black, Latinx, Asian, or multiracial. All the children with IEPs were children of color. Ms. Shima was an Asian American educator with fifteen years of teaching experience, and Ms. Davis was a Black educator with seven years of teaching experience. When I observed in their classroom, Ms. Shima and Ms. Davis were in their first year of working as a team, but they had a strong partnership that was evident in the loving, familial way that they communicated with each other and the seamlessness with which they shared responsibility in the classroom.

As they developed their classroom community together, Ms. Shima and Ms. Davis were committed to organizing their classroom using the principles of UDL. Their school had partnered with a consulting agency that worked with educational contexts to support inclusion of children with disabilities. Ms. Shima and Ms. Davis regularly attended trainings with this agency and met with a coach who helped them with their classroom setup and instructional implementation. From start to finish of each school day, the children in Ms. Shima and Ms. Davis's classroom experienced pedagogy that was universally designed. For almost every learning activity, the children were given the choice of modality of expression; independent work was broken into individualized chunks that reflected the unique goals and development of each child; they experienced varied grouping structures (e.g., pair, small group, whole group); and they had opportunities to meet individually with their teachers throughout the day. Giving children many options for how they would engage with the learning was a characteristic hallmark of this classroom.

Because the teachers had intentionally designed the classroom to foster multiple means of engagement, their toolboxes were incredibly full, making it possible for them to offer in-the-moment choices to children as needed. When it was time for children to engage in independent reading, they had options for digital, audio, or hard-copy texts. Throughout the day, children could choose among sitting on the floor, on a wobble stool, in a chair, or on a floor lounger with an attached desk. Often, children were given the option to complete work independently, with a teacher, or with a peer. Here is an example of how the classroom was structured in ways that incorporated multiple means of engaging in learning:

> The children were sent to different stations around the room for an English Language Arts block. One group met with Ms. Shima in one corner of the room, while another group met with Ms. Davis in the opposite corner. The third group went over to a laptop cart to pull out laptops and headphones. They took their devices to a cluster of desks and worked on a digital literacy game independently. At Ms. Shima's station, many of the children sat on floor chairs that curve in a way that allowed the children to lean back and that had little lap desks attached to them. Other children were seated on cushions on the floor. Still others were sitting upright in desk chairs. At Ms. Davis's station, children mostly sat on the floor in a circle around an easel where Ms. Davis was positioned. Several minutes into the lesson, a couple of children got up from the floor, walked over to a cart by the easel, grabbed a fidget toy each, and then sat in desk chairs that they moved close to the circle.
>
> Ms. Davis's group was working on a rhyming exercise. Ms. Davis would give them a word and the children would brainstorm words that rhymed with the given word. They wrote these down in a journal

they used for English Language Arts. Ms. Davis had readily available other materials for the children to create words as well. To one child who could not find his notebook, Ms. Davis gave a small whiteboard and dry erase marker. To two other children, she handed magnetic boards with letters that they could move around to create words.

At one point, a child groaned and pounded her fist on her notebook. "What happened?" a peer asked the child. "I don't know how to spell my word," the child said. Ms. Davis asked the group, "Has anyone else had that happen, where you struggle to spell a word that you're trying to write? Show me a thumb if so. You can show an actual thumb or an invisible thumb." Most of the children put their thumbs up. "What do you do when that happens?" Ms. Davis asked. The group then shared strategies they use, such as looking at the letter-sound charts in the room, stretching words out to hear the different sounds, and using sound motions to help them remember what sounds go with which letters. Ms. Davis checked in with the frustrated child and asked if she thought that any of the strategies shared would help. The child nodded yes and continued to work in her notebook. While the group worked on generating their lists of rhyming words, Ms. Davis left to go check in on the children who worked on their laptops independently.

In this scene, we see that the children in Ms. Shima and Ms. Davis's classroom were able to engage in English Language Arts learning in a variety of ways. The teachers broke the class into different groups to ensure more individualized attention to all the learners. Throughout the week, the children rotated through each station, allowing them to engage in the literacy focus for the week through a variety of lessons and approaches. In each group, children had the choice of where and how they would sit and participate in the learning experiences. Children used the flexible seating options, choosing for themselves how they wanted to position themselves in each group. They also had fidget toys available for them to use as needed. The varied grouping structures, seating options, and fidget tools all served to enhance children's engagement in the learning experiences.

We also see that the children were able to conduct their work using a range of tools. In addition to their English Language Arts journals, children were able to use whiteboards and dry erase markers or magnetic boards with magnetic letters. This variety was helpful for children who had more difficulty with executive functioning and frequently lost materials (e.g., their journals), as well as for children who struggled with letter formation and therefore preferred not to write by hand. The various structures, tools, and systems in the room were made available to all the children, regardless of whether they had an IEP, and indeed all children used and benefited from the resources and routines in the room.

When I asked Ms. Shima and Ms. Davis to reflect on how they provided multiple ways of engaging in learning, Ms. Shima said the following:

> We use these structures to really figure out how to support students and focus on their academics or behaviors, as opposed to, like figuring out, "Oh, why is this student always having a hard time getting their folders?" I would like to think that it comes from the growth mindset and not the deficit mindset, like, "Oh, they can't do anything." Instead of that, we try to phrase it as, "OK, this is not working, we need to figure out a different approach." So that's kind of where all this comes from. And, you know, like, the table arrangements too, and the optional seating, all of that. "What are the systems that are in place, or that we can put in place that support the students?" As opposed to "How am I going to make the students stop doing this?"

In Ms. Shima and Ms. Davis's philosophy, the classroom environment needed to be organized in ways that promoted access to learning for all children. When things were not working, rather than fault the children, they looked to see what in the environment could be changed or what they could shift in their own practices to better support each child's learning. It was this mindset that encouraged them to try many different tools. Ultimately, they developed a tremendously large toolkit in their classroom.

The resourcefulness of the room was reinforced in the conversation among the children at the end of the scene described here. When the children shared the multiple resources that they used in the room to help them with spelling, they highlighted how the classroom was set up in a way that intended to support all children's access to learning content and processes. Ms. Davis also positioned the children themselves as potential resources. She paused the lesson and made time for the children to support their peer, first conveying that everyone in the group had times when spelling felt hard, and then brainstorming strategies to use in those moments of struggle. This was a pedagogical move that cultivated *respect not restriction* by honoring struggle as a valid part of the learning process and embracing multiple strategies for working through that struggle.

Welcoming all forms of engagement for Ms. Shima and Ms. Davis also sometimes meant giving children the freedom to take breaks whenever the children themselves felt they needed them. There was a Peace Cart in the classroom, which stored a number of resources and tools that children could use if they felt they needed a way to get centered and calm themselves: sensory motion bubblers, fidgets, charts for identifying feelings, journals and art supplies, and timers, among other items. Throughout the day, children would go to the Peace Cart to pull tools they needed or to request a break from their teachers. One day, I observed as Amari, a Black boy with a history of trauma, got up in the middle of a math lesson and grabbed a folder from the Peace Cart. He approached Ms. Davis with the folder and filled out a chart that said, "I need _____ for [one minute, five minutes, ten minutes]." In the first blank, the child is to choose what option he wants for the break. Then he selects for how long he wants to take that break. Amari chose a book for ten minutes.

On that same day, Robert, another Black child with an IEP for Other Health Impairment (ADHD), went up to Ms. Shima holding a timer from the Peace Cart. The following occurred:

Ms. Shima looked up at Robert and asked him, "Do you need this right now?" The class was engaged in morning independent work, which involved completing a set of problems from a math workbook. Each child had a different set of problems that they were to complete.

Robert replied, "Yes," looking at his teacher with a steely gaze.

"OK, how much time do you need?" Ms. Shima asked.

Robert said, "Two minutes." Ms. Shima then set the digital timer to two minutes and handed it back to Robert. Robert went to his desk and sat in his chair, staring forward. His peers continued to do their work, and some chatted with one another; but everyone left Robert in peace.

Once the two-minute timer went off, Robert hit the stop button, took the timer back to the Peace Cart, and then went back to his desk. He proceeded to open up his math workbook and complete his assigned independent work.

What struck me most when I observed this moment with Robert was how much trust the teachers had in the children. When Robert approached Ms. Shima with the timer, she did not question him. She trusted that he needed the break he was requesting, and even gave him full say over how long his break would be. Once she set the timer for him, she left him to monitor his own break. As soon as his two-minute break was done, Robert was ready to do his work. This same kind of trust was shown to Amari, who similarly was able to dictate when he needed his break, what he would do during the break, and how long his break would last.

Trusting the children is what made it possible for Ms. Shima and Ms. Davis to build break-taking into the structures and routines of the room. Offering a break was not a reactive practice, something provided in response to children's behavior. Rather, breaks were one of the many tools and resources embedded in the classroom for children to manage their own learning processes. While in some classrooms, taking a break is something that an adult imposes upon a child as a consequence for undesired behavior, in Ms. Shima and Ms. Davis's classroom, taking a break was a welcome practice that children chose for themselves to maximize their own learning.

When I asked the teachers about their Peace Cart and break-taking structures, Ms. Davis shared, "In some of the students, and it can go for anyone, we recognize that there's a bigger need there, like a social-emotional need. We have to address that first, before we are shoving things at you. I feel like that's one of the things that has really helped with both Robert and Amari." Ms. Davis articulated an underlying principle that drove Ms. Shima and Ms. Davis's approaches to welcoming all forms of engagement with learning: children need to feel whole and well to be able to learn. By giving children ownership over how, when, and at what pace they learn, the teachers respected their whole beings. Restricting them to engage in narrow ways and within strict time frames would cause unwanted stress that ultimately impedes children's ability to learn. The expansive resource-rich nature of Ms. Shima and Ms. Davis's pedagogy made it possible for their children of color with disabilities—and all their peers—to know that their true and whole selves belonged in their inclusion classroom.

EXPECTING AND TRUSTING CHILDREN TO TAKE OWNERSHIP OF THEIR LEARNING

Underlying the pedagogical approaches of the DisCrit-aligned educators I've presented so far is their ability to trust children to take ownership of their own learning. Gloria Ladson-Billings (2009), in her Culturally Relevant Pedagogy framework, speaks of the importance of maintaining high expectations for children of color.[4] While the concept of "high expectations" is defined in varied and sometimes conflicting ways, the teachers I observed who enacted DisCrit Pedagogy held high expectations of their children, trusting that they would guide and make important decisions about their learning. *Respect not restriction* was enacted by giving children more freedom to learn in the ways that they themselves desired. Sometimes this meant creating structures and systems to offer children a good deal of choice in terms of how they engaged in the learning processes, as was the case in Ms. Shima and Ms. Davis's room. Other times, it meant letting children pursue learning in their own way, even when their actions fell outside the typical routines of the classroom.

Letting go of existing routines to free children up to take ownership of their own learning was a *respect not restriction* practice that was initially challenging for kindergarten teacher Ms. Soto. At the time I visited her class, Ms. Soto had close to twenty years of experience teaching early childhood. Her class included twenty-six five- and six-year-olds, six of whom had IEPs, and two paraprofessionals. One paraprofessional was assigned as a one-to-one support for Oscar. Oscar was one of the many children in the class who identified as Latino and was bilingual in Spanish and English. His family migrated to the US from Mexico several generations earlier, so both he and his parents were born in the US. When I observed Oscar in his classroom, he had an IEP for Multiple Disabilities and Speech or Language Impairment. Oscar moved in ways that seemed to indicate strong receptive language skills, where he understood a majority of what was communicated to him by adults and peers. He did not communicate using verbal language, however, and instead communicated mostly through his body and vocalizations that included shouting, humming, and grunting.

Oscar's favorite activity was drawing. Any time he had the opportunity to work with paper and markers, he would sit for hours making lines and shapes in different colors all over his paper. His passion for drawing became the source of some tension between Oscar and Ms. Soto. She was a teacher who believed strongly in the importance of nurturing children's autonomy. Her pedagogical philosophy was that children learned best when they were engaged in authentic inquiries facilitated by project- and play-based learning. Ms. Soto's school had, however, over the years become a more test-driven setting. Year after year, she received training on various programs that she was then evaluated on by her administration. Ms. Soto often told me that she was "not allowed" to teach the way she used to, as she needed to adhere to the "strict rules" that the school had established.

Over time, her experiences with top-down evaluation at the school shifted her own comfort level with children driving their own learning experiences. She began to internalize rigidity and a desire to control the children in her classroom. This was particularly evident during center time. Although Ms. Soto used to have time for children to engage in play-based centers, her centers had evolved to become solely literacy and math based. Children were not allowed to choose their centers but were instead assigned centers to go to. When I asked Ms. Soto whether children could move from center to center as they desired, she replied:

> They pretty much just stay at the center. What I'm trying to do is like letting them go—Like if they need their resource, like how to build a word, I tell them, "It's OK, you can go." So they'll go to the board, and they'll come back. . . . Or they'll go up to the board and write the word and then they'd come back. I'm like, "It's OK, you can go use your resources." They're like OK, and they're like looking at me. But that's the only time [they move].

Here, Ms. Soto described an environment where the children needed to seek permission to move around the room. Indeed, even when they received this permission, they seemed to look back at the teacher to confirm her approval. The only time movement was permitted was if a child needed a resource. Otherwise, children were meant to stay at their assigned center for the duration of center time.

Ms. Soto rotated the children so they were in different centers each day. Her reasoning was for children to "work on different skills throughout the week. I also like to mix up strong students with ones that need help because that's a good way to get that peer learning." Ms. Soto felt having such structured centers was especially beneficial for children like

Oscar because "you know, he was really aggressive. He's gotten a lot better." Ms. Soto believed that her center rotation system made it possible for Oscar to interact with a wide range of children and receive help from his peers, strengthening his comfort level with the other children in the classroom. This system of rotating centers was something that Oscar often resisted, however. He glowed when he was assigned to the writing center, with a wide grin on his face and a pep in his step as he hurried to the table with paper and markers. When he was sent to any other center, though, he showed the kind of behavior that Ms. Soto and other adults described as "aggressive."

Here is an example of what tended to occur when Oscar was sent to a center other than writing:

> Ms. Soto walked over to the center chart hanging on her wall and began to move children's pictures around. There was a quiet buzz among the children waiting on the rug. Several sat up on their heels and tried to see what their teacher was doing, eager anticipation filling their bodies as they wondered to which centers they would be sent. When Ms. Soto turned around, she called the first group: "Oscar, Estelle, and Luis, you are going to the literacy puzzle table." Oscar's paraprofessional helped Oscar up from the rug and walked him over to the puzzle table. Rather than sit in a chair at the puzzle table, though, Oscar walked over to the writing center, which was just a few feet away from the puzzles. He promptly sat down at the writing center and began to draw using marker and paper.
>
> Oscar's paraprofessional went over to the writing center, held Oscar's wrist, pulled him up to standing, and then walked him back over to the puzzle table. Oscar wriggled away from the paraprofessional's grasp and ran back over to the writing center. He quickly grabbed his marker and paper again and proceeded to draw. When his paraprofessional returned to his side, he let out a loud scream and threw a pack of markers at her. His paraprofessional then put her arms around

Oscar, picked him up, and said, "You need a break." She proceeded to carry Oscar out of the room, as he kicked his arms in the air, screaming and crying the whole way out.

After several instances like this, Ms. Soto said to me, "Something needs to change. I need to let go of something." She recognized that Oscar was showing behaviors of distress because he wanted to be at the writing center. His paraprofessional was beginning to express feelings of burnout as well because of the physicality of those moments of tension with Oscar.

Ms. Soto did not feel that she could let Oscar go to the writing center every day. It still felt important to her that the children follow the routine of the classroom, which was that their centers would rotate and the teacher would assign them to a different center each day. She was, however, willing to let Oscar take his writing and drawing materials to whatever center he was assigned to. His paraprofessional would then work with him on the assigned center's task by incorporating drawing and writing, or she would let him draw and write to stay grounded while they worked on the assigned task. For example, at the literacy puzzle center, Oscar and his paraprofessional created letter puzzles using marker and paper, which he would then cut up.

Over time, Oscar no longer had moments of tension during center time with either his paraprofessional or Ms. Soto. Many other children began to also take paper and markers from the writing center to their assigned centers, finding ways to connect writing to what they were doing. They made books using the consonant-vowel-consonant (CVC) words they created using magnetic letters at the CVC center. They drew pictures to go along with their number lines and Unifix cubes at the math center. They created signs at the audiobook center, reminding their peers to be quiet when they were over there. "It's amazing, what they're doing," Ms. Soto reflected. "Sometimes they still ask me if they can go get the paper, and I have to say, 'Yes, you can,' but what they're doing, it's all them." I, too, was impressed with how Ms. Soto's growing trust of the children made it possible for them to enhance their own learning experiences.

This transformation of center time occurred because of Oscar. Ms. Soto saw that trying to restrict Oscar led to his repeated exclusion from the classroom and unnecessary strain between him and the adults in the room. She decided that she needed to trust him more—trust that he could take ownership of his learning even if it was outside the boundaries she had established. When she trusted Oscar with the writing materials, he not only flourished, he also helped the other children in the class see that they too could guide elements of their own learning with just some paper and markers. By responding to Oscar with trust, respecting him rather than restricting, Ms. Soto positioned him as a leader in the classroom, thus cultivating a culture of belonging for him and all who learn like him.

As time went on, the children stopped asking Ms. Soto for permission to move materials around the room during center time. A shift happened as Ms. Soto trusted the children more and the children felt that they were trusted. Ms. Soto expected the children to truly own their learning, and the children in turn met those expectations. In this way, she enacted a DisCrit Pedagogy where children of color with disabilities are seen as full of assets, capable of doing much, and therefore worthy of trust.

ACTING FROM A PLACE OF GENUINE AFFECTION, LOVE, AND CARE

The pedagogical approaches described in this chapter would not be possible were it not for the genuine affection, love, and care that the teachers felt toward their children of color with disabilities. These sentiments were communicated to the children through the teachers' words, tone of voice, hugs, and authentic smiles, all of which told the children how much their teachers enjoyed them. This is not to say that the DisCrit-aligned teachers never felt frustrated with their children of color with disabilities. The relationship between teacher and child is just like any other relationship between human beings, and the potential to hurt one another is always present. What I noticed in teachers who enacted a *respect not restriction* pedagogy, though, was that even when they felt hurt, disappointed, angry, or frustrated, they maintained a desire to understand the children and ensure that the classroom environment was a setting in which the children felt that they could be their true selves.

I'd like to offer two contrasting examples that to me illuminate how acting from a place of genuine affection, love, and care can promote a DisCrit Pedagogy as opposed to a medical model–aligned one. There were two fourth-grade classrooms I observed in where in each class, there was a Black boy with an IEP for Other Health Impairment (ADHD) and Emotional Disturbance, who sometimes jumped on the desks in the room and moved his body through dancing, jumping, kicking, and making other big movements. In one classroom, when the child, Carter, jumped on the desks, he would be physically restrained by a teacher or some other adult in the building who would forcibly remove Carter from the classroom. Carter thus experienced punishment, exclusion, and stigma. One day, I entered the classroom and the teachers said to me, "We're going to have a great day today. Carter is not here, so it's going to be a good day." They announced this with all the other children present, so Carter's peers heard how the teachers felt about his absence. Even the assistant principal popped her head in that morning, noticed that Carter was absent, and said, "Oh it's your lucky day!" When Carter was present, he was often given an iPad on which he would watch YouTube videos. The teachers told me that they did this to try and keep him from exhibiting undesired behaviors, like climbing on the furniture.

The exasperation, frustration, and resignation that the teachers in this room felt was understandable. It can be extremely challenging when children's behaviors do not fit within our adult expectations and we feel concerned about the safety of all the children in the room. What had happened over time, though, was that the teachers saw Carter as a problem to be extracted, rather than as a child worthy of being loved just as he is.

In contrast, in the second classroom, the teachers responded to their student, Kyle, with genuine affection, love, and care, making it possible for them to enact a *respect not restriction* style of practice. Here is a description of one moment I observed:

> Kyle was up on a table, jumping and screaming out, "I'm king of the world!" Two children who were sitting at the table screamed in surprise and got up from their seats, backing away from the table.
>
> A teacher calmly walked over to Kyle and asked, "What do you need right now? What's going on in your body?"
>
> Kyle laughed and then exclaimed, "I'm gonna punch something!" Another teacher called the rest of the class over to a different side of the room and led them in a movement break exercise.
>
> "We're doing a movement break right now. Would that help you?" Kyle's teacher asked him. Kyle did not respond, but he stopped jumping. He began kicking materials off the table slowly with his foot. "Here, I have a pillow that I will bring to you. You can punch the pillow for three minutes, and then you can join everyone for the movement break," Kyle's teacher said. "But I need you to come down so I can give you the pillow."
>
> Kyle paused, looked at his teacher, and said, "I'm going to punch it really hard. It's gonna explode!"
>
> "That's fine," his teacher responded. "If there are feathers everywhere, though, we'll need to clean it up." The teacher reached out his hand to Kyle. Kyle took it, came down from the table, then walked with the teacher over to the group. The teacher gave Kyle a pillow to punch while everyone else continued with the movement activity. Eventually, Kyle also joined the group's movements.

In this moment with Kyle, we see how his teacher responds to his behavior from a place of genuine affection, love, and care, from the moment the teacher approached Kyle with a question: "What do you need right now?" This question communicated to Kyle a *respect not restriction* mindset. The teacher wanted to know how to support Kyle in this moment. His goal was not to control him. It is very possible that Kyle's teacher felt frustrated and exasperated with him. In fact, during our interview, Kyle's teacher told me "I definitely thought to myself, 'Oh, not this again!' But then I have to step back and remember that he's telling me something is not working for him." Because this teacher was not trying to change Kyle, but was instead trying to understand him, the teacher was able to enact a DisCrit Pedagogy where a need for a physical break was honored, and that physical break could involve punching just as Kyle had requested. Kyle's behavior actually inspired the other teacher in the room to offer movement to everyone, thus normalizing the act of expressing a need for a break.

Respect not restriction can take place only when teachers love their children of color with disabilities just as they are. When they do not see it is as their job to change children, but rather position themselves as adults who are trying to support children to be their full, true selves. As Ms. Campbell said at the beginning of this chapter, "You have to love them." When we are in relationship with people we love, we want them to thrive even when it feels hard, and even if we feel hurt by them. This kind of relational love is necessary for a DisCrit Pedagogy to be enacted with children of color with disabilities. You can offer an expansive pedagogy full of *respect not restriction* only if you truly love children and are invested in them, knowing that they are loved. In her book, *All about Love: New Visions,* bell hooks quotes psychiatrist M. Scott Peck as follows: "Love is an act of will—namely, both an intention and an action."[5] It is intentional, active love that makes *respect not restriction* possible so children's true selves can be embraced and honored.

4

Making Room for the Unexpected

WHEN THE DISCRIT-ALIGNED TEACHERS I observed showed *respect not restriction* with their children of color with disabilities, they often also enacted a practice that I call *making room for the unexpected*. This is a DisCrit Pedagogy move where the educators approach the children with curiosity, pay attention to the children's interests and ideas, and then create opportunities for the children to pursue those interests and ideas by providing requisite materials, time, and space. *Making room for the unexpected* is a form of power sharing, where children are positioned "as agents of knowledge production" and the gifts that they bring to the classroom are pursued as important resources that guide learning.[1] Teachers who *make room for the unexpected*, therefore, enact assets-based pedagogies, seeing strengths where others might see deficits, and building on those strengths to guide their interactions and instruction with children of color with disabilities.

In this chapter, I share four examples of how DisCrit-aligned educators *make room for the unexpected* to cultivate pedagogies of belonging in their inclusion classrooms. The pedagogical examples range from a small moment with a group of children to larger class projects that run for extended periods of time. In all the examples, the teachers were themselves surprised by the unexpected gifts that children of color with disabilities showed when the teachers made room for these gifts to be expressed.

A CHILD-LED EXPLORATION OF BEADS

When the eighteen three- and four-year-olds in Ms. Lopez's Spanish-English bilingual Head Start class entered their classroom each day, they found different materials waiting for them at each of the four tables in the room. Ms. Lopez explained in our interview, "I try to be really intentional with my materials each day because, you know, they are all in different places with their development and their interests. I think about things that will challenge and draw them in and that also connect to the curriculum." When she set up her classroom at the start of the day, she had in mind particular uses for each material that was laid out, knowing that she would be supporting children's growth and development in specific areas. As a Head Start inclusion teacher, she felt pressure to ensure that children were meeting their developmental targets and individualized education program (IEP) goals. "In our community, we're always talking about making sure our kids don't fall too behind. It's those fears of those gaps when you're working in a low-income community with language learners and kids with disabilities," Ms. Lopez told me.

Ms. Lopez, therefore, thoughtfully planned out morning table work that was multimodal, multisensory, and also fun. On one December day that I observed in her room, Ms. Lopez had set up the following tables:

- A hot chocolate–making center, where children worked with an assistant teacher to follow visual instructions and make hot chocolate.
- A holiday card center, where children used paper, scissors, markers, staplers, and tape to create seasonal cards. Children also made snowflakes at this table that they affixed to their cards.

- An audiobook center, where the children read and listened to books about winter.
- A beading center, where the children threaded beads onto strings to create decorations for the classroom in honor of the winter holiday season.

Through these various activities, children were able to work on their emergent literacy, fine motor, auditory processing, executive functioning, and visual processing skills in ways that were fun, engaging, and relevant to their context.

Despite Ms. Lopez's highly intentional and targeted planning of the children's morning table work, there were times when the children strayed from these plans. Take, for example, the following moment from my observation:

> After removing his jacket and putting it in his cubby, Tomás wandered over to Monica, who was working at the beading table. Monica had placed a tray in front of her and put some beads on it from the large bin of beads at the center of the table. She held a piece of string in her hands that she carefully threaded through beads one at a time. She held each bead close to her face as she worked to fit the end of the string through the bead's hole.
>
> Tomás looked at Monica's tray and took a large crystal-like bead off of it. Monica looked at him and opened her mouth, but then closed it and went back to focusing on her own bead and string. Tomás seemed to inspect the bead, holding it close to his eyes, almost as if to see if it would be the right size to fit a string through. He then placed the bead on the table and spun it like a top. "Look!" he exclaimed while pointing at the bead, a wide grin on his face. Monica looked up from her work and saw the spinning bead.
>
> She giggled and took a bead from her own tray, placed it on the table and spun it like a top. "Mines did it too!" she said.
>
> Monica then took another bead and spun it around on her tray. "It's going faster!" she said. Tomás took a tray from the table and leaned

> over the bin of beads. He inspected the bin and pulled out beads of different sizes and colors. He began spinning the beads one at a time on the tray. He and Monica continued their bead-spinning exploration, exclaiming to each other different discoveries they made: "This one is hitting it!" "Mines is faster than yours!" "The smaller ones is so fast."
>
> One of the assistant teachers came over to Tomás and Monica. "I notice you are spinning the beads," the teacher said to the children.
>
> "Yeah, this one is really fast. It goes like this," Monica said as she spun her finger in the air at a rapid pace.
>
> "Show me," the teacher said. The children proceeded to show the teacher the different beads that they had spun while telling her about their discoveries. Then the three worked together to set up a competition of sorts, where they would see which bead won the award for being the fastest on the table and which won for being the fastest on the tray. Their table was full of laughter and squeals that you could hear from all around the room.

At the time of this observation, Tomás was a four-year-old child with an IEP for Speech or Language Impairment. His family spoke a combination of Spanish and English at home, although Tomás was considered English dominant. He received bilingual speech therapy services for his articulation and expressive language, specifically around word retrieval. Ms. Lopez described Tomás as a friendly child who loved soccer and other games and was very affectionate toward his peers.

In this scene, Tomás initiated an exploration with the beads that diverged from the intended purpose: stringing the beads to create holiday decorations for the classroom. I knew how much intentionality and care went into Ms. Lopez's planning of each table, and I was therefore pleasantly surprised that the teachers did not stop Tomás and Monica from their bead play. In fact, the assistant teacher encouraged the children's investigation with the beads, following their lead and allowing the center to transform as it did.

When I asked Ms. Lopez about this moment, she told me that while she had her own ideas for how the materials would be used, it was important to "listen to the children." She went on, "Tomás loves competition, so I'm sure that's why my assistant encouraged that. If we stopped him and said, 'No, that's not what you're supposed to do with the beads,' we would have stopped his critical thinking, his language, all these things that we want him to grow in anyway." Ms. Lopez recognized that Tomás's and Monica's bead exploration actually supported the fine motor development and hand-eye coordination that Tomás was working to strengthen: "You're using a lot of that muscle to pull out a bead, place it on the tray, spin it around. So, he's still hitting the goals. And he's also interacting with his peer, which is good for his language."

Ms. Lopez's willingness to let go of her own plans and follow the children's lead was possible because of the assets-based perspective she had of her students. She was able to identify the brilliance in their self-created exploration. This did not mean that she let go of the goals that she had set for her children. It meant that she saw how it was possible for the children to still meet those goals in their own way without necessarily sticking to her plan. Not only were the children meeting the goals that Ms. Lopez intended with the beading center, but they were meeting additional goals that supported the development of the children's language, critical thinking, and social-emotional skills. In my view, Ms. Lopez was a highly intentional, deliberate educator who still *made room for the unexpected* by following the children's lead and approaching them with trust. A more medical model–aligned educator might have seen Tomás's behavior as disruptive and off-task. Ms. Lopez, however, opened herself up to different possibilities and recognized that Tomás's initiative with his learning was actually supportive of his IEP goals.

Ms. Lopez did acknowledge, "If they were like throwing the beads around and hitting each other, this might be a different story. I don't think I would have just let them do that." I appreciated her saying this because it clarifies a common misconception that people may have of child-centered learning—that following children's lead means just letting them do whatever they want. This was not what Ms. Lopez was doing. Child-led pedagogy, to Ms. Lopez and her assistants, involved approaching the children with trust, a desire to understand, and an orientation to see their strengths, while still holding onto the goals set for them. In Ms. Lopez's classroom, then, *making room for the unexpected* required teachers to know the purpose of their plans and the children's goals intimately so they could meet children's behaviors with curiosity while still cultivating their development with intention. This was particularly important in Ms. Lopez's Head Start inclusion context, where there was much pressure to ensure that children were hitting developmental goals in a timely manner. By following Tomás's lead from a place of high expectations, Ms. Lopez and her assistants actually *made room for the unexpected* targeting of goals beyond what they had initially planned, all the while promoting a climate of inquiry, joy, and belonging for children like Tomás.

WHAT'S THE NEWS?

"We've got to figure something out. It's like he's not a part of the class," Ms. Francis said to her co-teacher, Ms. Marques, reflecting on Jelani, a Black child with an IEP for Other Health Impairment (ADHD) in their second-grade inclusion classroom. Ms. Francis and Ms. Marques were both experienced Black inclusion teachers in an urban school that served an entirely Black, Latinx, and Arabic community. Over 90 percent of the school qualified for free and reduced-price lunch, and about a third of the students had IEPs. There were nine children with IEPs in Ms. Francis and Ms. Marques's classroom in the year that I worked with them; Jelani was one of those children. Jelani had developed a reputation as a "problem child" throughout the school. From the start of the school year, he was frequently sent to the principal's office for various behaviors: hitting and/or kicking peers, throwing objects or furniture, exclaiming expletives, yelling at teachers, or refusing to follow directives. Eventually, Jelani resisted going to the principal's office and would instead throw himself onto the floor. The assistant principal would come to get him, and a power struggle would ensue. As Ms. Marques put it, "You would hear him screaming and hitting Ms. Smith from two floors down. He was famous!"

Ms. Francis and Ms. Marques worked with the school administrators to come up with a reward system for Jelani. If he joined a class task for a certain amount of time, he would be able to watch a short video on the iPad. Over time, this reward also became a source of tension with Jelani, as he had somehow found a way to watch violent videos on the iPad. He then refused to transition away from the iPad once the allotted time to watch videos ended. "By January, I just gave up," Ms. Francis explained to me. "I couldn't keep fighting him. So, we just let him stay on the iPad." As inclusion teachers, Ms. Francis and Ms. Marques felt conflicted about this move. On the one hand, they were happy that Jelani was no longer being physically removed from their classroom so frequently. On the other, they felt that he wasn't truly a part of the class, even when he was physically there, because he stayed on the iPad all day.

By the time that I observed in Ms. Francis and Ms. Marques' classroom, though, a transformation had taken place in Jelani. He did still spend long chunks of the day on the iPad, and there was also one instance when he was forcibly removed from the classroom after he cursed at an administrator. For the majority of the time that I was observing, however, Jelani participated in class activities, engaging with his teachers and peers with interest and motivation. The change came about because of a particular project that Jelani's teachers allowed him to pursue—one that became an extended inquiry for the entire class.

> "Welcome to the Daily News, coming direct to you from Room 1-206." Jelani sat up straight and held up a stack of papers as he looked ahead at the camera. "My name is Jelani Jordan."
>
> "And I'm Chrissa Williams. Today we have breaking news from the White House."

Chrissa and Jelani proceeded to take turns sharing important headlines from the day's news. They reported on the war in Ukraine, climate change, and ChatGPT, as well as on their own school's recent community fundraising event. After finishing their reports, Jelani said, "and now for the news in sports. Take it away Julio." He pointed towards his left, where Julio was standing wearing a Lakers jersey. Ms. Francis pointed the camera in Julio's direction, as Julio gave a rundown of the NBA and college basketball victories the night before.

Meanwhile, there were children sitting at a cluster of desks with laptops open and pieces of paper scattered in front of them. Ms. Marques sat with them, helping them with their research and supporting their writing. Some children wrote sentences that describe important stories from the news while others drew important news events. There were also children wearing headphones and watching news clips on laptops. Groups of children were assigned to different parts of the news: weather, sports, national headlines, international headlines, and school news. They attended to their work with tremendous focus and zeal.

Every day for thirty minutes, the children in Ms. Francis and Ms. Marques's second-grade inclusion classroom were invited to participate in a class "news station." Children who did not want to participate could work on independent writing and art projects. Each day, though, at least half of the children chose to contribute to the news station. The news station project was an inquiry that Jelani had inspired. During my interview with the two teachers, Ms. Francis told me, "The school has its own news thing, and one day, Jelani was asking me about it. So, I showed him some videos and he was like, 'Oh, I wanna do that.'" Ms. Marques continued, "I told him, 'Well you've got to work for it.' He said, 'I want to be an anchorman,' so I was like, 'OK. Well, you got to do XY, and Z, then you can be, you know? And I'll record you.' So that's how it started." Ms. Francis went on, "I recorded him and then everyone wanted to be recorded. But when it was their turn, they didn't really know what to say. So that's when the research came in." "That's right!" Ms. Marques continued. "Julio wanted to be the sports anchor and he's really good at it, I believe. And River wants to anchor too, and she is really shy and struggles with speech. So, this is good for her to work on her speaking, her language."

As the teachers told me the story of how the news station began, their own energies were up and their enthusiasm was high. "He came up with the idea," Ms. Francis said about Jelani. "He came up with the idea and then I just said, 'If it was to come to life, where would it go? What would we need? Where will it live?' And then he started giving us ideas. So, it really came from him. But now all the kids love it." Ms. Marques added as she reflected on Jelani, "Before, I thought he was a kid who was just busy. Very, very busy. He's here, he's there, he's just busy. But this particular kid, if he puts his mind to something, he will actually deliver. I don't think he understands that when I tell him. This, he really put his mind to." While both teachers did continue to have some deficit-based beliefs about Jelani (e.g., "He can't listen," "He doesn't know how to control himself," "I think he acts out because learning is too hard for him") and at times conveyed a pathologizing perspective of his behaviors (e.g., "I think he needs medication to calm down," "He should probably see a counselor about his obsession with violence"), Ms. Francis and Ms. Marques also came to appreciate how following Jelani's lead allowed them to see a side to him that they had not seen before.

When I observed Jelani in his news anchor role, I never would have imagined that just a month prior, he had been pulled out of the classroom on a daily basis for punitive reasons. I saw in Jelani a leader in the classroom, who felt tremendous ownership over the daily news project. He was not excluded, isolated, or pushed out in the way that he had been before. As his teachers made room for Jelani to explore a genuine interest, he became more invested in engaging with the learning of his classroom. As they became aware of Jelani's many talents and capabilities, his teachers also became increasingly invested in supporting his interests and inquiries in the classroom. This then made it possible for them to create opportunities for other children, both with and without disabilities, to also pursue their interests and develop skills through the classroom news station.

By listening to Jelani's questions and following his interests, Ms. Francis and Ms. Marques *made room for the unexpected.* They launched a class project that engaged not only Jelani, but most, if not all, of his peers in the class as well. The classroom news station completely transformed Jelani's behavior and positionality in the classroom and school. He was no longer seen as a "problem child"; instead, he was valued as an important leader and contributor to the classroom. He also went from being perpetually excluded from the class to being a vital member whose ideas were respected and acted upon. Ms. Francis and Ms. Marques were able to *make room for the unexpected* in this way because they felt committed to authentic inclusion. Although they felt stuck and unable to continue during their initial power struggles with Jelani, they also did not want his existence in their classroom to be one characterized by exclusion.

In addition to this commitment to inclusion, the teachers saw themselves as co-learners with their children. As Ms. Francis said in a one-on-one interview that I had with her, "The kids, they teach us a lot of things. Sometimes we think because they're not doing what they're supposed to do, they can't [teach us], but we learn from them. They're teaching us also." It was this learner's stance that opened Ms. Francis and Ms. Marques up to *make room for the unexpected.* Jelani was very much one of the kids that other adults might see as "not doing what they're supposed to," and therefore unteachable. Even though Ms. Francis and Ms. Marques also slipped into pathologizing views of Jelani, they still believed that he was capable of teaching them. When they created space to listen to him and follow his lead, the entire class benefited. The news station project was one that engaged a majority of the children. It promoted belonging among the children in the inclusion classroom because they truly owned this piece of the curriculum. Jelani and his peers shone in unexpected ways because Ms. Francis and Ms. Marques listened and followed.

RELATIONSHIP-BUILDING WITH DIALOGUE JOURNALS

Starting in the middle of the schoolyear, the thirty children in Ms. Corey's fourth-grade inclusion class—eight of whom had IEPs—began each Friday morning with journal writing. This was a time when they could write about anything at all. "I just want them to write," was what Ms. Corey told me when describing this time of day. Her hope was that by getting into this regular habit of journaling, children would have an easier time writing during the class's writer's workshop. She noticed that many of her children had a hard time getting started when it was time to write, so she thought that the Friday journal time could help them develop a writing habit. The school where Ms. Corey taught was majority Chinese immigrant and was considered a Title I school. Her inclusion class had a significant number of children labeled "English learners" who were either Cantonese speakers or Spanish speakers. "Writing freely, with no expectations placed on them, I think helps them make it less intimidating. There's no right or wrong," Ms. Corey explained.

At the time that I was observing in Ms. Corey's classroom, Jessica was one of her Cantonese-speaking children labeled "English learners," who had an IEP for Specific Learning Disabilities. Jessica had emigrated to the US from China with her mother, father, and baby sister three years prior. She was a child who had strong linguistic capabilities in Chinese. Her bilingual special education teacher was often impressed with Jessica's Chinese literacy skills and speaking abilities ("She can read and understand Chinese newspapers!" she once exclaimed to me). Her progress in English was an area of concern, however, which often led the specialists working with Jessica to wonder if her academic difficulties were truly related to her learning disabilities or were tied to her acquisition of English. Perhaps because of Jessica's strong abilities in Chinese, she conveyed much frustration when she had difficulties in English in her classroom. As Ms. Corey told me:

> Wednesday morning, they were writing narratives, and she was trying to remember how to say 'roller coaster' in English. She was really frustrated that she didn't know. It was hard. I could tell she was frustrated because she was trying to explain it to me but didn't have the language to explain it to me, so I couldn't access the word for her. When things like that happen, it's frustrating for her. She knows what she is thinking of but she doesn't know how to describe it to me, so I can't help her with that.

I observed Jessica during one of these moments of frustration. She was reading with a paraprofessional, Ms. Lisa, during independent reading time. Jessica read aloud to Ms. Lisa, and Ms. Lisa stopped Jessica periodically to support her with her decoding of vowel sounds in particular. For example, when Jessica read the word "original," Ms. Lisa stopped her and had her repeat each syllable after her a few times. Jessica had both of her hands clenched around the edges of her skirt. She pulled and squeezed the fabric with a seeming nervousness, biting her lower lip as she listened to Ms. Lisa enunciate each syllable. After a while, Jessica looked down at the table and stopped repeating after Ms. Lisa. Ms. Lisa asked, "Are you nervous?" while looking at Jessica's hands on her skirt. Jessica shook her head "no" while continuing to look down at the desk. Another child leaned over to Jessica and said, "original." Jessica jolted upward, hit the child in the face, and exclaimed, "Don't talk to me!" She then ran out of the room, squatted in the hallway, and cried while exclaiming, "I'm trying my best! I'm trying my best!"

These types of emotional expressions were common for Jessica at the start of the year. She frequently ran out of the room in distress because of her frustration with her work or with a peer. This started to change midyear, once Ms. Corey instituted the Friday morning journals. The Friday morning journal time became an important place for Jessica to convey all that she was feeling and experiencing. It also allowed her to practice writing in English without her usual frustrations of worrying about spelling or trying to find the correct words. While Ms. Corey's original intent with her Friday morning journal time was to get children into the habit of writing, she came to see how this modality of expression allowed her to better understand what was going on for Jessica internally. The following are several entries from Jessica's journal. Much of the spelling has been changed to fit Standard English norms, as I was hastily writing the words in my field notes journal and did not think to preserve Jessica's original spelling at the time:

Entry 1: *I like being young. You grown-ups have so much to worry about. You have to worry about rent and work and house. I just have to worry about me and school. I don't want to get old.*

Entry 2: *My mom and dad's friends come to our apartment. They played a game. Then my mom and dad yell at each other. I don't know why. My dad smoked and talked to his brother on the phone. I did not sleep.*

Entry 3: *Everything was better in China. Here, things are not fun anymore. In China, my grandfather and grandmother and uncles and aunts were all fun. My dad is not fun. I don't like what he says to my mom. But I am like my dad. I get angry and talk like him.*

"Before we did the journals, I never realized how self-aware and deep her thinking was," Ms. Corey told me. As Jessica was a child with an IEP for Specific Learning Disabilities and an "English learner" designation, her educators often focused on supporting her with her language and literacy skills to get her "caught up." This led to a deficit-based view of Jessica. Ms. Corey, however, started seeing the maturity in Jessica's social-emotional development and awareness, as well as in her understanding of the world around her. Ms. Corey also grew in her empathy toward Jessica. "I used to call her 'sensitive,' but now I see it's more than that," she reflected to me one day.

Ms. Corey did not typically respond to her students' Friday journals because she wanted this to really be her students' time, but with Jessica, she felt that a response would be helpful, especially given how personal Jessica's entries were. She wrote notes back to Jessica such as, "Thanks so much for sharing this, Jessica. It sounds like you miss China. Can you tell me more about what you love about China?" and "We grown-ups do have a lot to worry about! I think kids have a lot to worry about too. What do you do when you feel worried?" These responses invited Jessica to respond to her teacher, and the two engaged in a written dialogue through these journals. Every Friday, Jessica would enter the classroom with a hurried step and rush to her desk, where her journal waited for her. She would read Ms. Corey's response and then work on crafting her own.

After a few weeks of this, Ms. Corey told Jessica that she didn't have to wait until Friday to write in her journal. "I said to her that I would put her journal on her desk each day along with the morning math work. If she wanted to write in her journal before starting her math, she could do that," Ms. Corey explained to me. Indeed, every day, Jessica came into the classroom and started with her journal writing. Often, she still had enough time to then at least start her math work as well. Having this space to communicate with her teacher through writing seemed to put Jessica at ease each day. She started showing fewer moments of frustration in the classroom and was also more comfortable asking her teacher for assistance throughout the school day. When a peer did something that she did not like, Jessica would go straight to her journal and write something down. It proved an important outlet for Jessica, which made it possible for her to stay present in the classroom, both physically and mentally, and engage in the learning processes with her peers.

Ms. Corey *made room for the unexpected* with Jessica by responding to the communication that Jessica was giving her through her journal entries. "I realized, she just needs someone to listen to all the many things that she is holding in her head," she said. When Ms. Corey started to respond to Jessica's whole being, recognizing and responding to her social-emotional development as well as her academics, Jessica came to see the journals as an important outlet. This outlet made it possible for her to get through her days in the inclusion classroom without having big emotional expressions that would lead to her leaving the room. The journaling also opened the door to Ms. Corey talking to Jessica's family about having Jessica speak with a counselor on site about the many things she was dealing with. Jessica's mother ended up agreeing to family counseling as well, which led to significant transformations for Jessica in terms of how she expressed her emotions in school.

"Sometimes when students have an IEP for one thing, we get so focused on that that we forget they have other things going on in their lives too," Jessica's special education teacher, Ms. Xi, told me in our interview. Ms. Corey leaned into the relationship-building that Jessica seemed to invite through her journals. As with Ms. Lopez, Ms. Francis, and Ms. Marques, Ms. Corey followed her student's lead and responded with curiosity to *make room for the unexpected*, ultimately engaging in dialogue journaling. The dialogue journals allowed her to establish a strong coping mechanism for Jessica, help Jessica feel known and seen, and refer Jessica for additional services that supported her emotional and mental health. "I think for a long time, she was trying to tell me something that I just didn't recognize until we started writing to each other," Ms. Corey reflected. "It was like I really saw her clearly for the first time."

THE EMERGENT TEXTILES PROJECT

At the time of my data collection in her classroom, Loretta was a five-year-old Black kindergartener in an inclusive classroom led by two teachers, Ms. Russo and Ms. Gallagher, and one paraprofessional, Mr. Taylor. The school was in an urban district that served a majority of students of color (each school in the district was made up of over 60 percent students of color), most of whom were Latinx and Black. A total of 40 percent of the students in the school had IEPs and 35 percent qualified for free and reduced-price lunch. While the school did not have much information on Loretta's home life, they knew that she lived alone with her father, who had custody of her, and that she was able to see her mother on some days. There was a history of drug addiction in the family's past that the school knew very little about. Kindergarten was Loretta's first schooling experience. There were twenty-three other children in her classroom.

Loretta was in the process of getting an IEP for Emotional Disturbance. She was a child with many interests, especially artistic ones. Loretta loved the sensory experiences of getting her hands dirty with paint, glue, clay, and other materials. She also had a lot of interest in movement, making big jumps, running, and dancing in any environment, indoors or outdoors. Loretta at the time was on the smaller side in her class, but her emotional range was very large. She expressed her emotions—negative or positive—with a loud voice and many physical movements, like kicking or pushing with frustration as well as jumping with enthusiasm. Although small in stature, Loretta had a very large presence.

One of her teachers, Ms. Gallagher, described the first days of school for Loretta in the following way:

> She was very bright, very enthusiastic, very energetic, but was having a very hard time connecting to people. Since her first day in our classroom, Loretta struggled with being comfortable and regularly demonstrated this by running away, kicking, pushing, slamming, jumping around, screaming loudly, talking over teachers, having loud tantrums, and refusing to do what the rest of the kids were doing. She wasn't used to having other adults in her life, and it didn't look like she had a ton of experience with other kids either. She called me "Yellow" for the longest time. She got the kids' names, but the adults were called not by their name until she felt like really settled here. The whole environment was just an unfamiliar, strange place for her to be.

After a few weeks in the classroom, Loretta took a liking to Ms. Gallagher in particular. Ms. Gallagher then took the lead with supporting Loretta.

From the beginning of the year, Loretta frequently ran out of the classroom. Ms. Gallagher said about this time period, "Loretta did not want to stay in the classroom. She found the classroom really restricting, and we have one of the biggest classrooms!" Although the classroom had several places where children could go to get some alone time, as Ms. Gallagher put it, "That wasn't helpful to her. She was just uncomfortable and constantly moving her body. So, for like the first three weeks, she would just run." Loretta ran through the hallways, up and down the stairs, around the cafeteria. A teacher always went out after her and tried different approaches to coax Loretta back into the classroom. The teachers would text each other after a given amount of time to trade places if one person's approach wasn't working. As Mr. Taylor told me one day when Loretta had made a run for it, "Each of us has our own styles and approaches with her, so sometimes we have to just rotate in and out to get her to come back."

For Ms. Gallagher, her approach was to start pointing out artwork around the halls. As she told me:

> One of the things that I did is we would look at the art in the hallways. We would look at whatever was on the walls, and I would try and see what engaged her. Figure out what she was interested in, or what she saw, or what she was getting out of this time. And eventually, if I allowed her to do some of that, that would give her what she needed. Then she would actually voluntarily take my hand and come back to the classroom, and we'd join the rest of her classmates.

When I asked Ms. Gallagher why no one at the school ever seemed to try and physically force Loretta to come back into the classroom, she said to me, "I've seen people handle kids who are experiencing stress in that way, and I know it doesn't work. It just exacerbates the situation." She also said, "In any other setting where I've worked, Loretta would have been described as disruptive, dangerous, and out of control. Everything would have been handled punitively, without ever giving an opportunity to understand her or see her fully. Not here." For all of Loretta's teachers, they wanted to respond with humanity and curiosity, not with punishment, because they understood that Loretta's behavior stemmed from her own discomfort in the classroom. They gave Loretta the space that she needed to eventually make her way back to the classroom.

Ms. Gallagher, however, also wanted to engage Loretta in such a way that whatever seemed to ground her in the hallways could be transferred into the classroom. On one of Loretta's runs out of the classroom, Ms. Gallagher did exactly what she described to me. She spent about thirty minutes in the hallway trying to encourage Loretta to come back to the classroom. Ms. Gallagher began looking at the artwork and pointing out her observations to Loretta. Eventually, Loretta also started to point to artwork that stood out to her. For instance, she pointed to one particular art piece that was created using wool. "One of the things that she found in the hallway was this fiber art landscape," Ms. Gallagher explained, "It was just like multicolored pieces of roving stuck on a piece of cardboard and framed, you know, and she was fascinated by it."

When Loretta made her way back to the classroom, the children were in centers for work time (or what other schools might call "center time" or "choice time"). Loretta went over to the art center and got some masking tape. Ms. Russo saw this and recalled, "She was frantically working with this material. It was clear that she had some kind of vision. Or she had some kind of thing that she was really trying to show us and teach us. And I realized she was trying to re-create the amazing thing she had seen in the hallway." Ms. Russo shared this with Ms. Gallagher, who had a background of working in textiles. This sparked Ms. Gallagher's creativity. She decided to develop a fiber arts project for the class. A few days later, the children began this project. They studied the process of making wool, different textures, and eventually created their own wool art pieces using yarn, glue, and cardboard. The teachers made sure to emphasize that this project was inspired by Loretta's discovery, and they often asked Loretta to help them demonstrate different elements of the project.

One of my observations in Loretta's classroom took place during the emergent textiles project. Loretta's enthusiasm for the curriculum was palpable. When Ms. Gallagher introduced a classwide exploration that they were going to do with pieces of wool roving, Loretta frequently jumped up from her seat and squealed. Children were sent in groups of two to three to select roving and begin a fiber project with water and soap at tables. When it was Loretta's turn to go up, she practically leaped across the room to make her selections. Then the following ensued:

> Loretta went over to Ms. Gallagher, who was holding a basket full of different strips of fiber. She thrust her hands into the basket and squeezed fistfuls of the roving. "Pick just three to start," Ms. Gallagher said. Loretta pulled her hands out of the basket and selected three different strips. She then walked over to a table with Mr. Taylor. Mr. Taylor stayed with Loretta throughout the activity to support her with each step. Ms. Gallagher gave the children instructions that they followed one by one as the teachers went around the room to provide individualized support. There was a joyful buzz at the tables, as children scrubbed their fibers and got their hands covered in soapy foam.
>
> About ten minutes into the experience, Loretta began shaking. Foam from the soap had reached up all the way to her elbows. She held her hands up towards her face. Her elbows were bent and her whole body quaked. She was making a high-pitched sound from her mouth that wasn't quite a scream, nor a cry. Mr. Taylor asked Loretta if she was all right, but she continued to shake. He then held Loretta's shoulders and walked her over to the classroom sink to wash her hands. It took Loretta several minutes to stop shaking. She and Mr. Taylor eventually read a book together on the rug. When they finished, Loretta walked around the room to see her peers' creations.

Ms. Gallagher admitted that she was disappointed that Loretta did not finish her project. She, Ms. Russo, and Mr. Taylor reflected that perhaps the project's sensory nature was overstimulating to Loretta; she might also benefit from working in a smaller group.

The teachers decided to have the children continue their textiles exploration as a center during work time. Ms. Gallagher planned to lead children in creating a fiber art piece similar to what Loretta had seen in the hallway. When Loretta chose the textiles project center, the following took place:

> Loretta and three other children—Max, Lexi, and Jack—came over to the table where Ms. Gallagher was seated. She had a stack of small cardboard rectangles, a basket of roving, scissors, and glue laid out on the table. Ms. Gallagher reminded the children that their textiles project was inspired by Loretta's discovery in the hallway. "We're going to begin our time together by going into the hallway and looking at the fiber painting that Loretta found for us."
>
> Loretta let out a long, high-pitched scream as she plopped down onto a chair, slamming her fists onto the wood and flopping her torso to lay flat on the table. Jack yelled out, "Stop!" and covered his ears. Ms. Gallagher responded, "Loretta is angry about having to go into the hallway to see the picture. She wants to get straight to work. Jack is upset by the noise and it's bothering his ears. Why don't we all sit at the table, and we can figure out a time to go see the picture in the hallway after we finish the project." The children nodded and took their seats at the table. Loretta slowly eased herself up to a seated position in her chair.
>
> Ms. Gallagher then went over the materials and gave instructions for how to create their individual fiber paintings. As the children began their work of gluing the yarn onto their cardboard, Loretta continued to work with the glue on the cardboard. With a mesmerized expression, she experimented with dabbing the glue with a stick, squeezing it from a container, dripping it into small and large blobs, and spreading it over and over into different smatterings all over the cardboard. She left it to dry, and then returned to her cardboard piece to add additional glue using a variety of methods. As she worked, she sang a little jingle and shook her body in a small dance. She never once touched the yarn or experimented with it at all. Ms. Gallagher left Loretta to continue with her glue explorations.

Throughout the textiles project, Loretta did not actually work very much with yarn. Although it was her interest in the fiber painting that had sparked this extended project for the class, Loretta was drawn to other materials besides yarn, which were somewhat unexpected for the teachers. "We kind of realized that she needed more time to discover material that might be new," Ms. Gallagher reflected. Every day of the project, Loretta would be fascinated with a material or tool and would "immerse herself" in whatever that material or tool was, as all three teachers described it. She took scissors to cut up pieces of felt over and over again. She sorted buttons. She counted threads. "It became about giving her space to have new experiences," Ms. Russo shared. For a child who had never been to school before, the textiles project gave Loretta time and space to explore and become comfortable with newness. During this project, she never once ran out of the classroom, and after the project, those incidences of running continued to decline.

I love so much about Loretta's journey in her kindergarten inclusion classroom. Ms. Gallagher and her team showed deep humanity and care, as well as a dedication to making the classroom a place where Loretta would feel like she belonged. They *made room for the unexpected* several times, first by launching the textile project based on Loretta's fiber painting discovery, and then by following Loretta's lead in terms of how she wanted to participate in the project. Ms. Gallagher admitted to feeling disappointment at various points throughout the project because she thought that Loretta would engage in all the activities that she had planned, exactly as she had planned them. Instead, she learned to "let go," as she put it, and pay attention to what Loretta was communicating to her. All the teachers ended up seeing that Loretta just needed a way in to becoming comfortable in the classroom. Exploring newness was the theme for Loretta throughout the textile project, and that allowed her to feel more grounded in herself and comfortable in the classroom.

DisCrit Pedagogy cannot be separated from this idea of belonging because it is only when children of color with disabilities, like Loretta and the other children described in this chapter, feel like they belong that they can meaningfully engage in learning. *Making room for the unexpected* is about following children's lead, being genuinely curious about what they are communicating and thinking, and having an expansive view of what it means to learn so the children feel a sense of ownership and belonging in the classroom. Loretta and all the other children described in this chapter were able to guide their learning in ways that felt meaningful to them because the teachers responded to them with openness, care, and a desire to understand. As a result, the teachers learned things about their children of color with disabilities that they themselves never expected, and they got to facilitate learning experiences that were richer than they could have imagined.

When I asked Ms. Gallagher what she thought Loretta gained from the textiles project, she said:

> She learned how to trust other adults. That people genuinely care for her and that she can care back for them. That relationships can be safe and reciprocal. That she has a lot to offer. I think she feels like she has a role to play. She's part of a community, but she brings unique, compelling, interesting, valuable, important things to the table. I think she feels like maybe a new kind of awareness of how important she is. And how creative and capable.

Making room for the unexpected in Loretta's class meant that Loretta showed sides of herself that surprised the adults and her peers, but she also came to see herself in ways that were surprising to her as well. While Loretta questioned at first whether she belonged, her teachers were committed to ensuring that she *knew* she belonged, just as she is. This commitment led to the creation of an environment where Loretta came to embrace her belongingness. And she no longer needed to run.

5

Centering Inquiry

IN ALL THE STORIES I've shared so far of DisCrit Pedagogy in action, educators *centered inquiry*. Inquiry involves asking questions to gather information, which often leads to both action and additional questions to pursue. An inquiry is authentic when the individual pursuing it is genuinely curious about the answers to the questions that they have. In early childhood, inquiry-based learning means "a path of learning that follows children's interests."[1] This path of learning involves asking questions, defining problems, developing models, planning and carrying out investigations, analyzing and interpreting findings, and sharing thinking/learning in some way. When learning is guided by questions, inquiry emerges and the path of learning unfolds.

Centering inquiry is a practice that I observed occurring in two primary ways. The first was through the educators themselves adopting an inquiry stance toward their children. We see this in how Ms. Allen interacts with Mario in chapter 3, as she showed genuine curiosity in the butterfly that he created during the children's poetry work. We also see this in the assistant teacher's response to Tomás and Monica's bead play in Ms. Lopez's room in chapter 4. Rather than shut down the children's play, the teacher was curious to learn the children's intentions, so she invited the children to tell her about their exploration. Ms. Shima and Ms. Davis in chapter 3 also adopted an inquiry stance as they experimented with multiple learning structures and modalities to see which ones helped to facilitate learning for all their students. DisCrit Pedagogy thus requires that teachers be authentic inquirers into and information gatherers about their children.

This inquiry stance is a necessary precursor to the second manifestation of *centering inquiry* that I observed: the educators created environments where children could pursue their own inquiries. The way that Ms. Francis and Ms. Marques in chapter 4 set up the news station in their second-grade classroom, inspired by their own inquiry into Jelani, is an example of teachers *centering inquiry* for children of color with disabilities. Ms. Gallagher's textile project with Loretta in chapter 4 is another example of an educator creating opportunities for children to pursue inquiry. This project emerged from Ms. Gallagher and the other teachers working to understand Loretta's interests and ways of being. When teachers are curious about their children of color with disabilities, they authentically engage in investigations that can spark creative ideas that will facilitate the children engaging in inquiries themselves. *Centering inquiry* is, therefore, a DisCrit pedagogical practice that involves both inner work and external action on the part of the educator—the inner work of taking a stance of curiosity toward children of color with disabilities, and the external action of creating opportunities for authentic, child-led inquiries for their children.

In what follows, I share four examples of educators who *centered inquiry* into children of color with disabilities. These examples show us how *centering inquiry* is a DisCrit pedagogical practice that elevates the gifts of children of color with disabilities and facilitates their belonging.

THE CHILD SAFETY LOCK INQUIRY

> If I see a child that's not a part of our community, I really sit down, I do research, I try to figure it out. I partner up with the therapist, I'm like, "Hey, he's doing this. What do you think we can do? How can we work out something to have him come further into the classroom?" I want him to be a part of our community. And, it was just trying to figure him out, and just taking the time to get to know him, observe him, take down the data, and just say, "OK, you know what? He likes to see how things work. So, let's bring something into the classroom that's gonna pique his interest, and see where it goes from there."

These words, from preschool teacher Ms. Reyes, reflect both the inquiry stance that she took toward children and the mentality that she applied to the inquiry she created for three-year-old Ian. Ian was a Puerto Rican and Dominican preschooler with autism in Ms. Reyes's class of twelve Black and Latinx children ages three and four. His year in Ms. Reyes's class was the first time that he had ever attended school. Ms. Reyes told me that Ian was primarily surrounded by adults and much older siblings at home, so he was not accustomed to being in a room full of children. "For the first month or so, he wouldn't come into the classroom," she explained. "The closest he would come is right by the door. He would hold onto the edge of the door and the doorknob. The door would open. And he would listen to the click of the door and close it and then open it and close it. He's very, very smart when it comes to how things work."

After several weeks of observing Ian, Ms. Reyes saw how he was a child driven by inquiry. He was curious to explore different materials and learn how they work. Ms. Reyes decided to try and find objects that Ian would be willing to explore further inside the classroom, rather than solely at the door. She started by putting out different-colored Velcro circles in various places of the room—on shelves, rugs, bins, and other materials. Ms. Reyes described the moment that Ian first discovered the

Velcro circles: "When he saw the colors, he immediately wanted to go, and he started ripping them off. Then he started putting them back on. So that's how I got him midway into the classroom." The Velcro served as an initial way to get Ian to move his exploration of how things work from the classroom door to halfway into the classroom.

To bring Ian even further into the classroom, Ms. Reyes bought a "busy board" block, which had a faucet, wheel, light switch, door latches, a window, and other tools that Ian could explore. She placed the block in what Ms. Reyes called "the creative play area," which was past the center of the room. During the class's choice time, Ian would wander over to the block and explore the tools on it for several minutes. He would then get up and head back to the door of the classroom. Ian was now spending longer stretches of time inside the classroom, but he still spent most of his day right outside the classroom or standing by the classroom door.

Ian's exploration with the busy board block inspired a new idea in Ms. Reyes. As she put it, "I knew that in order for me to get him further into the classroom, I needed something that he can play with. Something that he can open and close that would keep him occupied." And so began Ian's inquiry with the child safety lock straps:

> Ian creeps toward the tables at the back of the room, watching Ms. Reyes and her assistant intently as they model opening and closing the child safety lock straps attached to the table. There are two straps affixed to the top of the table, each facing a different direction. "This is so much fun!" Ms. Reyes exclaims while pulling a buckle off of one of the straps. When he arrives at the table, Ian observes the teachers' actions but does not touch the locks himself. This is the second day that Ian has come this far into the classroom to observe the safety lock play.
>
> After observing for a few minutes, Ian reaches out his hand toward the locks. "Do you wanna try?" the assistant asks Ian. Ian remains standing but begins exploring the safety lock straps on the table. He squeezes the buttons on the side of one buckle. The strap pops up,

> and Ian inspects the edges of the buckle. He pushes the end back into the holder that is stuck on the table and listens for the click. Then he squeezes the edges again and watches the strap pop up once more. As Ian continues his investigation, a teacher brings over a snack since the class is currently in snack time. "Have some pretzels, Ian," the teacher says. Without looking, Ian takes a bite of his snack, his gaze focused on the strap on the table as he continues to snap the buckle in and pop it out.
>
> When the class transitions to circle time at the end of snack, Ian stands up and walks over to a closet in the classroom where another safety lock strap is attached to the closet door. Ian plays with the buckle and strap as the class engages in a group song and dance. Suddenly, he hears a song turn on that seems to spark a light in Ian. Ian stops his exploration of the child lock and wanders over to the rug to join his class. With a wide grin on his face and energy shooting down from the top of his head all the way to his toes, Ian participates in the singing and dancing. When the song ends, he leaves the rug and walks back to the child lock on the closet door to continue his exploration.

As time went on, Ian became increasingly comfortable walking straight into the classroom, sitting down at a table, and engaging in his child safety lock play. Gone were the days when he clung to the door and would not enter the classroom. Ms. Reyes also used the song that he enjoyed as a way to invite him into the class's circle time. By a couple of months into the year, Ian was spending the entire day in the classroom, engaging in the majority of the activities that his peers did. When he was not with the group, he remained close by, exploring with his child safety lock straps to continue his inquiry into how things work.

Like all the other DisCrit-aligned educators whose stories I've shared so far, Ms. Reyes was a teacher who was committed to a fundamental belief that all children belonged in her classroom. Ian's experience with exclusion was more internal than externally imposed. He did not initially feel safe in school and therefore needed support to find a way into his class community. The way in that Ms. Reyes found was to *center inquiry.* She set up various inquiries for Ian that built on his interest in exploring how things work. She began with the Velcro inquiry, then moved on to the busy board block, and finally landed on the child safety lock straps as a way to encourage Ian to enter the classroom fully and stay with his peers. A natural investigator, Ian was drawn to the inquiries established for him and began to see the classroom as a place where his interests and explorations mattered. At no point did Ms. Reyes force Ian to do anything in the classroom. His engagement in various activities were self-motivated and driven by his own interest, curiosity, and inquiry.

For Ms. Reyes to enact the DisCrit pedagogical practice of *centering inquiry,* the other two practices of *responding with respect not restriction* and *making room for the unexpected* needed to be in play. When I asked her why she never forced Ian to come into the classroom when he spent so many weeks just hanging on the door, she told me:

> If I was to do that, I was going to take away the child's autonomy to make the decision to come in. I have to wait for him to make me a part of his world. He wasn't ready yet. It took weeks. This is not something that happened overnight. This was something that took weeks, months. It was tiny little baby steps to get him further and further into the classroom. . . . I knew I had to allow him to make his way into the classroom. And I do that with all the children. I don't force them. I don't grab them. I don't restrain them. I don't pick them up. . . . That would be me not giving him the respect. I have to respect his body and respect his space. . . . I think about it that way. Like, how would I feel if a grown-up or someone bigger than me was restricting me and putting me in a place I don't want to be. That's gonna make me more frustrated. And I didn't want to give him a bad first impression of what my classroom would be like, because had I done that, he would not want to come to my class every day. He would not want to be a part of our community.

Ms. Reyes explained that if she were to restrict Ian further and try to force him to enter the classroom on her terms, school would have felt like an even more unsafe place for him. Instead, she *respected* Ian and *made room for the unexpected* by observing him and following his lead, trying various things in the hopes that he might act upon the inquiries that she established. As she said, "I mean, the worst thing that could happen is that it wouldn't have worked out. And I would have had to go back to the drawing board and figure something else out."

We see in the example of Ian how *centering inquiry* means both giving children experiences to engage in inquiry to gain a sense of belonging in school and approaching children of color with disabilities from an inquiry stance. Inquiry rooted in children's interest was fundamental to Ian's sense of belonging in the classroom. In his first weeks of preschool, the only thing of interest to Ian was the classroom door. It allowed him to engage in an exploration of how things work, whereas crossing the threshold of the entryway meant exposing himself to a scary, unfamiliar space. Once he found opportunities to pursue how-things-work inquiries in the classroom, the room felt like a more exciting and interesting place in which to be. Creating an inquiry-centered learning environment for Ian was respectful of who he is as a learner and a human being. It gave him the autonomy to decide for himself when and how he would enter the classroom.

The establishment of the safety lock inquiry also demonstrated Ms. Reyes's own self-reflectiveness. She did not assume that her classroom, on its own, would be enticing to Ian. As she explained, she knew that she had to "wait for him to make [her] a part of his world." Ms. Reyes thus engaged in her own inquiry. She observed Ian, took in data, practiced some trial and error, researched potential materials that would spark his interest, and set up her environment in ways that would invite his inquiry. Ms. Reyes's inquiry *into* Ian helped her create an inquiry *for* Ian that ultimately fostered his sense of belonging in the classroom.

About a week into Ian's safety lock inquiry, I reflected with Ms. Reyes on how things were going. She told me the following:

> It's really amazing to see how far he has come. The other day, he put his forehead against my forehead, and I knew that he was saying, "it's OK. I trust you now. It's OK, I'm going to be a part of this community." . . . He comes into the classroom now. He participates, he's starting to be verbal, he's repeating things. When we sing, he's very excited, he screams, and it's just a beautiful thing to see him just open up in the way that he's opening up now.

When teachers like Ms. Reyes have curiosity toward children of color with disabilities, when they see them as capable beings full of strengths, they are able to *respect* children enough to *make room for the unexpected* by *centering inquiry.* When this happens, a sense of belonging is possible for children of color with disabilities like Ian.

CREATING SPACE FOR INQUIRY IN GUIDED READING

Whenever I walked into Ms. Daniel's mixed-age first- and second-grade classroom during their literacy block, there was a quiet buzz in the room. "I love to hear them talk about their thinking," Ms. Daniel told me when we debriefed my first visit to her room. "I don't like it when the room is really quiet." She taught a class of twenty-two first- and second-grade children, eight of whom had individualized education programs (IEPs) for a range of disabilities. Her class was quite linguistically diverse. She had a mix of Spanish-speakers, Vietnamese-speakers, Chinese-speakers, Tagalog-speakers, and Hindi-speakers in her classroom. A majority of the children were labeled as "English learners." One paraprofessional was assigned to the classroom full time, and two others rotated in and out of the class.

During reading lessons, Ms. Daniel and the primary classroom paraprofessional met with small groups of children to engage in guided reading groups while the rest of the class worked on independent reading. The guided reading groups were meant to focus on discrete literacy skills, such as fluency, various elements of phonics, comprehension skills like making predictions or inferencing, and vocabulary development. Ms. Daniel, however, felt that the guided reading groups were also a time when she could *center inquiry* with her children. "Especially my kids with IEPs for language-related disabilities, the last thing I want to do is discourage them from reading. All of my kids should love reading, you know? So, yes, we need to make sure they get the skills, but none of that will matter if they hate reading," Ms. Daniel said during our interview.

Ms. Daniel's desire to spark joy in literacy was especially true for first grader Huy. At the time I was working with Ms. Daniel, Huy was a six-year-old Vietnamese- and English-speaking child diagnosed with Speech or Language Impairment and Intellectual Disabilities. She suspected, however, that it was Huy's speech and language abilities that led to his receiving low scores on his psychoeducational evaluation and being classified under Intellectual Disabilities. Although Huy's family spoke Vietnamese at home and there was a Vietnamese-speaking paraprofessional who supported the classroom, Huy did not seem to communicate in Vietnamese, from what the teacher could tell. Ms. Daniel said of Huy, "he's a friendly, bright, and really social child who has strong receptive skills. His main difficulty is that he can't express himself in a way that other people understand because of his articulation. But his coping skills are amazing. He's really imaginative with his gestures and hand signals." The teacher went on to say that Huy played well with his peers, although sometimes he would get stuck during interactions with others: "He'll try to initiate play or interact, but his peers have a hard time understanding him so then they'll kind of walk away." Despite the language barriers that Huy experienced, Ms. Daniel saw him as a child with "a lot of potential academically. He's a really smart and engaged learner. He just can't get his ideas across in a way that people understand him. Even I have a hard time, and I've been with him all year."

When I observed Huy, I similarly saw a child with an incredible ability to communicate using his full body. He did indeed appear to understand everything that was said to him, and he demonstrated a strong interest in communicating his ideas and responding to others. The words that he uttered were expressed quite quickly, and in a high-pitched tone. He seemed to have a wide range of consonant and vowel sounds that he could make, but these sounds came together in ways that were not always discernable to others. When he spoke, he used his hands to point, make shapes, and get others' attention. He also acted things out with his entire body, as if he were choreographing the words that he spoke. Ms. Daniel recognized these linguistic strengths in Huy and wanted to create many opportunities for him to share his thinking with others. "I don't want him to ever feel discouraged," she told me, "That's my biggest fear with Huy. That one day, he'll shut down and won't speak because others don't understand him, or maybe even bully him for the way he talks."

It was for this reason that Ms. Daniel made sure that her literacy lessons incorporated open-ended read-alouds where children could engage in inquiry with texts. Ms. Daniel told me once informally following an observation, "Fluency, decoding, answering comprehension questions, these are all things that will make Huy lose confidence. My assessments, they don't capture all the great ideas he has. I don't want reading to be that for Huy." While she did follow the guided reading program and instruction of the school, she also peppered in these open-ended, inquiry-based text discussions so she could give Huy opportunities to use language and communicate his ideas without any judgment.

Here is an example of Huy's engagement with the book *The Snowy Day* by Ezra Jack Keats. Ms. Daniel decided to read this book after their community had experienced the first big snowfall of the season. Huy was in a guided reading group with three other first-grade peers:

> "He thought it would be fun to join the big boys in the snowball fight," Ms. Daniel read, "but he knew he wasn't old enough – not yet."

Ms. Daniel paused, looked up from the book at the children and said, "Tell me about what's happening here."

Huy replied, "I dee. Do they take it? They get hurt?" while he hit his own chest.

Ms. Daniel asked, "They get hurt?" seeming to clarify what Huy said.

Huy mimed holding a ball in his hand and then hitting it against his own chest as he said, "Oh they lo kee lo kuh day yeh. The white ball it goes guh they."

Ms. Daniel continues reading. She turns the page and reads, "So he made a smiling snowman. And he made angels." Ms. Daniel then asked, "Why is he doing that?"

"A star oh lee oh lee vee!" Huy exclaims. He stretches his arms out wide and begins flapping them.

"He's doing like this!" another peer exclaims, imitating Huy's arm motion.

A third child says, "He's doing it because he's happy!"

"Is he making a airplane?" Huy asks, as he leans his body to the left and then to the right while his arms remain stretched out wide by his sides. "This is a airplane," Huy says.

On the next page, Huy sees the illustration of the main character sliding down a snowy hill. "Wee!" Huy exclaims while waving his arms in the air. "I dey too slide. I down bey doh bide," Huy says.

"Wow. Yeah," Ms. Daniel responds.

"The slide!" Huy says while running his right hand down in a sliding motion in front of his chest.

"He's doing down huh," Ms. Daniel says.

"He go down," Huy continues, "down on the dowtain."

In this example, we see that Ms. Daniel created space for Huy to share his reactions to and thoughts about the text. Although she provided prompts like, "Tell me about what's happening here" and "Why is he doing that?" Ms. Daniel followed Huy's responses and let him pursue the inquiries that emerged from his reading of the text. He was given the freedom to explore aspects of the text that stood out to him. On the snowball fight page, Huy seemed to react to what he interpreted as the main character getting hurt. He saw the snow angel-making as the main character creating an airplane. Huy also concluded that the child was sliding down a snow mountain. He shared his thinking through his words, but also with his gestures and body movements. At no point was Huy corrected or asked to repeat himself. The point was not that he comprehend the text or answer the teacher's questions in a particular way; rather, the point was exploration of and inquiry with the book.

In several of my observations in Ms. Daniel's classroom, I saw that Huy was given space to react to texts in whatever way he chose. Imitating and acting out things that he saw in the illustrations were common ways that Huy made sense of the books that the group read. Ms. Daniel read many books that involved animals to the children because she realized that the group really loved animals. While reading *Bark George!* by Jules Feiffer, Huy reacted to a scene where a vet pulls a duck out of a dog by saying, "He's gonna eat tho la dee ga dee ga he go out it go ah gah." As he said this, Huy put his hand in his mouth and pretended to pull something out of his throat. As he pulled the imaginary duck out of his mouth, he said, "Wo do ee do dey."

Another way that Huy reacted to texts was by essentially talking at them. He would see things that sparked a reaction, either because he felt an emotion about something he read in the book or because he was making a prediction about what might happen next. When reading *The Mitten* by Jan Brett, a book that involves many animals getting inside a mitten left on the snow, Huy had a big reaction to the page where a bear approaches the mitten. "Oh no da big. Too big," Huy said while shaking his head and finger in the air. He went on, "Uh dala dai deh do wah dala big belly bey wa bada hand," and lifted his hand to show the group. Huy seemed to be saying to the group that the bear was going to be too big to fit inside the mitten. Ms. Daniel saw all these responses to the texts as inquiry. "Honestly, I don't always understand what he's saying," she told me. "But I know that he is making sense of the stories in his own way. And that's what I love about Huy and doing this with him. He is really curious and I just want him to keep that going."

Huy's freedom to engage in inquiry with texts was especially evident when he asked his own questions about the book rather than responding to the teacher's questions. For example, during one of my observations, Ms. Daniel read the book *Good Night Gorilla* by Peggy Rathmann. Midway through the story, there is an illustration where the page is completely black except for two big eyes. This page comes after an illustration that shows all the zoo animals lying in the zookeeper's bedroom getting ready to sleep. The zookeeper's wife says, "Goodnight Dear," and all the animals respond, "Goodnight." There is a monkey lying in bed next to the zookeeper's wife. The following ensued in the discussion with the children:

> "Whose eyes were they?" Ms. Daniel asks.
>
> "Oh no, what is that?" Huy asks, pointing at the book. He stands up and leans across the bean table to get close to the text. Another peer also stands up and leans toward the book to see what Huy is pointing to.
>
> "Look at what?" Ms. Daniel asks.
>
> "Look at the big monkey," Huy continues, "and they gonna gonna gonna gonna gonna gonna get the ju ju ju." He puts his hands in fists and pounds them against each other while looking at the book.
>
> "Oh, is she gonna get mad at the monkey?" Ms. Daniel asks Huy as if to make sure she understands what he is saying.
>
> "I'm mad," Huy says as he puts his hand into fists and makes a frowning face. "Right there, where they going," he continued. He leans forward again and points at the book.
>
> "What do you think?" The teacher asks this to another child at the table. "What do you think is gonna happen next?"
>
> "They're going to sleep together. That's why they say goodnight," one child responds.

"Yeah but she gonna get scared by the monkey in her bed!" another child says while laughing.

"Ju ju ju," Huy says, pounding his fists together again.

Instead of answering Ms. Daniel's question, Huy spontaneously asked a question of his own about something that he noticed in the text. While Ms. Daniel could have pressed him to make sure that he answered her question, she decided to follow up on his verbalization and let the conversation move in the direction that he wanted. With Huy's prompting, the group had a conversation predicting what might happen in the following pages of the text. Ms. Daniel's inquiry into Huy's ideas led to a group inquiry into the book.

Again, Ms. Daniel did not completely ignore the school's guided reading program. There were times when Huy and his group members read books that focused on particular phonics skills. Huy often rested his chin on his fists, with a frown on his face, as he worked to decode the texts and work on his fluency. In these lessons, Ms. Huy also did more redirecting of Huy to ensure that he answered the comprehension questions that she asked. Perhaps because there were these times when Huy had to attend to a narrow skills orientation to literacy, when he had the opportunities to engage in more inquiry-oriented reading discussions, Huy seemed to light up. His linguistic and sensemaking strengths really shone when he was given room to explore the texts in the ways that he desired, asking his own questions and responding to the stories with his varied linguistic repertoire. It was in the open-ended, inquiry-oriented reading experiences that Huy's self could really be seen and known.

PURSUING ONE'S OWN QUESTIONS IN THE MACHINES AND INVENTIONS STUDY

Any time we had peaches for snack, he'd say, "Peaches here are nasty." And he'd compare them to the peaches he ate in Georgia at his

> grandparents' house. There was one week where we had peaches for snack like every day. It was like the cafeteria staff were trying to get rid of all the peaches in the school or something. Every day he was talking about these amazing peaches he had in Georgia. And he was asking, "Why?" Like, "Why are they so bad here and so good in Georgia?"

This excerpt from an interview I had with Mr. Bundy tells the story of how second grader Calvin, a Black child with an IEP for Other Health Impairment (ADHD), launched a months-long inquiry into farming tools and his own family history. Mr. Bundy's class of twenty-one second graders, five of whom had IEPs and a majority of whom identified as children of color, was engaged in a long-term project on machines and inventions. Mr. Bundy applied an emergent curriculum approach where he and his students co-created thematic units that ran across multiple months at a time. He was, therefore, highly accustomed to *centering inquiry* with his students. "For me, one of the biggest challenges is coming up with a topic that's going to be broad enough to allow multiple points of entry," he explained. "Because not every kid is going to be like, 'Wow, I love peaches, I want to study that.' So, you need to come up with projects where every student will be able to follow their own mini-interest within the larger project. That's what we did for Calvin."

In many ways, the discovery of Calvin's questions about peaches was a relief for Mr. Bundy because he and Calvin were having a hard time coming up with a focus for him. "Calvin really needs to love what he's learning about. Otherwise, he won't participate," Mr. Bundy told me. For this unit of study, each child was to select a machine or invention to research and eventually present to the school community in an exhibit. While his peers had chosen inventions like the light bulb, printer, and vacuum cleaner, Calvin was feeling stuck. That is, until he asked his question about peaches. Mr. Bundy explained:

> I started to do research on what it takes to grow peaches in Georgia, and it turns out there are so many things that have gone into making

> Georgia the home of the perfect peach. From the plow to the box crates to the railroad to the brushing machines to hydrocooling technology. A lot of really neat stuff that I thought Calvin might be interested to learn about. He's really connected to his family in Georgia, too, so I thought, OK, this is a way to bridge home and school and like really lean into Calvin's interests.

What I observed in Calvin was most certainly a "spark" of sorts, as he seemed completely engrossed in his inquiry into the peach industry. Here is a description of a scene that I observed when the children were working on their blueprints.

> Calvin is leaning over his desk, his elbows propped up on the table as he draws on the chart paper in front of him with a pencil. He is sitting on his heels, his legs crossed at the knees and his shins resting on top of his chair. I walk over to Calvin and ask him what he is working on. He looks up at me wide-eyed and smiles as he says, in a high-pitched voice, "So this is the truck they use to till the soil to make sure it's ready for the peach trees. You have to use this special soil called loamy soil that makes sure the soil isn't too wet because otherwise the peaches won't grow that good." Calvin turns back to his paper and continues to draw. He then says, "My grandma said that the soil in Georgia is what makes the peaches there so good, so you have to really get the right soil. Not like the dirt stuff we got here."
>
> Calvin points to another part of his blueprint and says, "And this here is the truck that carries the crates for when you're collecting the peaches. They use the hydrocooling in the crates to keep the peaches at the right temperature. That's how come we can get peaches from Georgia here too, but they don't taste right. It's not the same." I ask him why it doesn't taste the same, and he lifts up his torso to sit up straight. He replies, "Because it's like if something is in the refrigerator too long just don't taste right. My grandma says it's like when you have meat in the

> freezer for too long and take it out. The meat isn't as fresh and tastes like the freezer. That's what happens to the peaches."
>
> Calvin goes on to tell me more about his blueprint and the different elements of Georgia peach-growing that he learned about. In the course of the conversation, it becomes evident to me that he has also spent a lot of time talking about his inquiry with his family in Georgia. At the end of our conversation, Calvin turns to me and asks, "Have you ever had a Georgia peach?" When I tell him that I think I've had peaches from Georgia, but I've never had one in Georgia, he says, "Oh, you gotta eat it there. You can visit my grandma and grandpa's house and they'll give you the best peaches."

Calvin and I went on to talk about the different ways that his family uses peaches in their food. I could see from our conversation just why peaches became an important inquiry for Calvin. His family was full of individuals with a history in the agricultural business. There were also several members of his family who seemed to be highly skilled cooks. They baked pies, made peach cobbler, and canned peach jam—much of their family activities together centered around the Georgia peach. In some ways, it seemed, the togetherness and connection that Calvin felt when he visited his family in Georgia was what he missed most up here in New York, where he lived with just his mother and brother. While peaches themselves were indeed of great interest to Calvin, it was what the peaches represented for him that really drove his inquiry.

While I focus here on Calvin, there were many other children in Mr. Bundy's class whom I could have shared about. All these children had unique inquiries that they were eager to pursue. Often during my observations, the children would be in a lesson where there were varying levels of engagement. Some children seemed to be very engaged in the lesson, while others participated, but with low levels of energy and perceived interest. When they transitioned to researching for their inquiry projects, however, the class would jump up from their seats and move quickly to get back into their individual investigations. All seemed highly motivated to learn what they could to produce a strong product that they felt proud of for the final exhibition.

I asked Mr. Bundy if what I observed in his classroom was pretty typical of his students. He said:

> Honestly, yeah, I think so. Our kids take a lot of initiative with their projects. I mean, it's really important that each of them feels a sense of ownership, which is why I try so hard to make sure all of their inquiries are tied to their interests. I'm of the mind that when kids are invested and interested in what they're learning about, then you're not going to see the behaviors that might drive a teacher nuts, and they end up sending them out of the class. I don't have that here. Calvin is a kid who if he's not interested, he'll let you know. And so, I make it a point to make sure he's got an inquiry that he's connected to and excited about. I think he would show behaviors otherwise, but I don't have that issue here because I don't ever let it get to that point.

Like the other DisCrit-aligned educators described in this chapter, Mr. Bundy's ability to create opportunities for inquiry for his students was rooted in his own inquiry stance toward the children. At the heart of Mr. Bundy's pedagogy was the belief that every child has an inquiry that they want to pursue. It was just a matter of finding it. For children of color with disabilities like Calvin, who might communicate a lack of interest in school through behaviors that might lead to exclusion, figuring out the right inquiry to pursue was the key to inclusion and belonging. Once Mr. Bundy found the inquiry that sparked genuine interest in the child, he set up opportunities to engage in deep, long-term investigation. Calvin's knowledge of the peach industry in Georgia completely blew me away. It was this *centering of inquiry* in Mr. Bundy's classroom that ensured that Calvin was fully invested in his learning. He got to pursue authentic questions that came from him and his own experiences, and all the while he came to understand that his questions and his inquiries mattered in his classroom.

PRIORITIZING PROCESS OVER PRODUCT IN THE HOUSE BUILDING PROJECT

Ms. Aguilar walks toward the front of the room and reaches into a closet as Ms. Diaz explains the task the children are about to engage in. "Clifford is SO big that we need to build a big house for him," Ms. Diaz explains. An audible gasp is heard throughout the room when Ms. Aguilar pulls out large cardboard boxes and tosses them into the center of the rug. The children start bouncing in their seats with excitement. Some even reach out to touch the boxes, eager to start their project.

The children start by making a plan. First, they must figure out how high the house will be. "We have to be able to reach it!" one child exclaims while standing up with arms reaching to the sky. "OK, so maybe about this high?" Ms. Diaz asks as she extends her arm to the point that the child was able to reach. "And how wide does it need to be?" Ms. Diaz asks. Ms. Aguilar and Ms. Diaz stand next to each other and ask if the house should be as wide as the two of them. The children then begin lining people up shoulder-to-shoulder beside the teachers and determine that the width of the house should be nine people long. The length should be "the whole carpet!" one child exclaims. "We have to work together" another child states.

The children then start grabbing the boxes and opening them up so that they make hollow squares. They look at each other, grinning and seeming to think about what they should do next. "What do we need to make them stick together?" Ms. Diaz asks. "Tape!" one child shouts. The teachers begin handing the children rolls of masking tape. The children get to work. A few children tug the tape back and forth from each other. Others pull the ends of their tape rolls to get long strips of tape out. Several children even use their teeth to cut pieces of tape off. They work together, some holding different parts of the cardboard while others stick tape to the boxes.

This inquiry into making a house came after Ms. Aguilar and Ms. Diaz read a book to the children about Clifford, the big red dog. The class was in a unit of study about homes and had engaged in several mini-projects related to books they had read that connected to this theme, such as *The Three Little Pigs* and *Mi Casa Is My Home.* On this day that I was observing, the project was an inquiry into building a home collectively that would be the right size for Clifford, the dog.

This was an inquiry that involved all eighteen three- and four-year-olds in Ms. Aguilar and Ms. Diaz's inclusion classroom. The Head Start program of which this class was a part was almost 100% Black and Latinx, and this was true of Ms. Aguilar and Ms. Diaz's classroom as well. In addition to the two head teachers, there were three paraprofessionals in the room, all assisting with this mini-project. Of the eighteen children, eight had IEPs. There was one child in particular, Aiyden, a Black child diagnosed with autism and considered to be "nonverbal," who frequently had an adult nearby. Aiyden was a child who communicated through gestures and big body movements. While he was given much freedom to move around the classroom and engage with materials and with his peers without adult intervention, either a paraprofessional or a teacher stayed close to him in case he moved his body in ways that could hurt himself or a peer. For example, I observed Aiyden on a few occasions climbing up on furniture, and an adult would walk over to encourage him to come back down to the floor. Or another time, I watched as Aiyden ran along the edge of the classroom with a pair of scissors in his hand. An adult caught up to him and put one hand on his shoulders to stop him as she asked him to hand her the scissors if he was not going to use them to cut something.

While Aiyden received more direct attention and intervention from adults than any of the other children, there was a sense in the classroom that he belonged just as much as everyone else. I saw this as being tied to Ms. Aguilar and Ms. Diaz's practice of *centering inquiry.* Returning to the house-building mini-project, we see that the children demonstrated investment as they generated a vision for the house and ideas for how to execute on that vision. In the execution process, all the children in the class participated, working collaboratively to hold up cardboard, cut tape, and assist one another with putting together the walls of their house.

Aiyden also participated in the inquiry, but in his own way:

> As one child attaches a piece of cardboard to the side of the structure with tape, they announce, "This is the door!" Aiyden walks over to the door, knocks on it, and then opens the door to walk through the doorway and into the house. Aiyden then walks back out of the house and continues with this action, repeatedly going in and out of the cardboard structure. "You're going to break it," another child says to Aiyden. Aiyden then comes out of the house and begins knocking on other parts of it. He sees a tunnel-like part and climbs through the tunnel, again going in and out of the house. "Stay out, Aiyden," one child says to him. "We're building a big house." Aiyden crawls out of the tunnel and continues to knock on the sides, sometimes pushing his whole body against the side of the structure. A few times, children tell him, "Stop!" but then he continues with his exploration. For the most part, Aiyden's peers leave him be.
>
> When the house is finished, the children cheer and begin exploring the different entrances, taking turns going in and out of the house through the door and the tunnel. There is an energetic buzz in the room as children laugh, squeal, and make exclamations with each other like, "Look at this!" and "Move!" In all of this energy, Aiyden runs around the structure, continuing to knock his body against the structure. At one point, he runs into the cardboard house with much force. "Oh no!" a few children exclaim, as Aiyden's body sinks into the cardboard and ultimately crushes the structure down into a collapsed state.
>
> "Oh, did making a house work?" Ms. Diaz and Ms. Aguilar ask. "No, it broke," one child says. "Can we try again?" another child asks. "Yeah, let's make another one!" a third child says in excitement. The children

and teachers decide to try making the house again during their afternoon work time. Some children continue to try and fix the house, adding tape to it. One child says that she is "adding a Band-Aid" and that "the house has a booboo."

What surprised me the most while watching this scene unfold was how the children responded to Aiyden's actions, expressing displeasure if that was something they felt, and then quickly moving on without making much of a big deal about what he did. When Aiyden went in and out of the house through the door or tunnel, some peers told him to stop, which he responded to without hesitation. As he explored the sides of the structure, his peers also asked him to stop, perhaps in worry that he would break the building. Ultimately, though, they essentially left Aiyden to engage in his own individual inquiry. It is difficult to know exactly what he was trying to explore. From my vantage point, it seemed as though he was curious about the structure and how well it was constructed; but it is impossible to know the purpose that Aiyden had for his inquiry. What was evident, though, was that Ms. Aguilar and Ms. Diaz had created an environment in which the community would accept that Aiyden had his own way of interacting with their mini-project of building a house.

The moment when the children's acceptance was most apparent was when Aiyden ran into the house and the structure collapsed. Without batting an eye, the children came up with the idea of building the house again later in the day. When I asked the teachers to reflect on this moment with the children, Ms. Aguilar said the following:

> A couple of the boys in the class, right now they're in the knock-down stage. They like to see things break. They love to see things tear and break and fall. The rest of the kids have come to terms with it. Like one of the boys will come and kick something and they're like, "That's not nice, but I can build it over," and they just keep going. So, it's not as upsetting to them because we've talked to them. "Right now they

> like things that fall." . . . The kids didn't understand that at first, but then they started seeing that he's actually, he likes that. So they'll build and if he knocks it down, they're like, "That's not nice, I'll just build it again." And they just turn around and build it back.

For Ms. Aguilar and Ms. Diaz, the outcome of building the house was not as important as giving the children the opportunity to engage in inquiries in their own way. We see in Ms. Aguilar's comment here that she recognized Aiyden's tendency to knock things down as part of a longer-term inquiry that he was engaging in—a "knock-down stage" where he could "see things tear and break and fall." As the children were engaging in their own inquiries of building, then, they were also encouraged to honor Aiyden's inquiry into knocking things down.

The children's acceptance of Aiyden's inquiry was facilitated by Ms. Aguilar and Ms. Diaz's focus on process over product. At the end of the day, the experience of engaging in the house-building mini-project was not about ensuring that the children had a masterful final product (although the house they created together was certainly impressive). What mattered most to Ms. Aguilar and Ms. Diaz was the learning that came out of the process of working on this project together. As Ms. Aguilar put it:

> They're listening to other children's ideas and combining them with their own. Understanding that even when kids have different ideas, they can work together. They might have an idea of what a house looks like, but somebody else's idea may be different. Like, "OK, well, it needs a chimney." Well, my house might not have a chimney, but another kid can show them what to do. They're learning empathy. They're learning that other people have different feelings and different ideas and that's OK. They're learning how to work together. They're learning acceptance that kids are different and that's OK. And coming to terms with the differences and realizing that even though they might have different abilities, they can still play with them and still work together. . . .

> They're realizing that we can make mistakes and saying like, "I'm upset but that's OK. I can just fix it." Being able to understand that it's OK to make mistakes because we learn from our mistakes, and that's going to help them in the long run.

For Ms. Aguilar and Ms. Diaz, *centering inquiry* meant zooming in on the process of engaging in inquiry because it was during the investigation process that children learned. The learning that came out of the process was not just about the main concepts of their unit of study on homes. The children's learning was also about what it means to be human alongside many different people who have different ideas, interests, experiences, and abilities from each other. In this context, where process was valued over product, every child's inquiry was seen as valid, even when they had conflicting priorities or outcomes. Aiyden's knocking-down inquiry was in direct opposition to the other children's inquiry into building a house. Yet everyone's inquiry mattered because the aim was not that children would have something to show the world as a result of their investigation. Rather, the goal was for children to learn what it means to be curious together, which meant accepting all ways of thinking, being, and investigating.

Ms. Aguilar and Ms. Diaz's DisCrit pedagogical practice of *centering inquiry* came out of their *responding with respect and not restriction* and *making room for the unexpected.* They honored all the children's interests, not seeing any one interest as being more valuable than another. They also did not try to force the children into any particular lines of inquiry. The teachers thus respected the interests and questions of all the children in their inclusion classroom. For Aiyden, this respect also manifested in the teachers giving him room to explore and move his body in ways that he saw fit, even as they kept a close eye on him to intervene only if something he did might cause harm to himself or a peer. Ms. Aguilar and Ms. Diaz also *made room for the unexpected* in their emphasis on process over product. They did not have in mind what the children were going to produce by the end of the mini house-building project. In many ways, whether they even had a house by the end of the project was of secondary importance. What the teachers cared about most was what the children learned in the process of working together to build the house. Ultimately, as the teachers *centered inquiry,* they made room for lessons around plans not working out and learning to try again.

In all the stories shared in this chapter, we see how the act of *centering inquiry* made it possible for the children of color with disabilities to feel a sense of belonging because the children's unique interests and questions were seen as important to the learning in the classroom. *Centering inquiry* was a way that teachers showed the children respect and made room for unexpected discoveries, learning, and growth to take place. The teachers were able to create inquiry opportunities for their children because they themselves were curious about their children of color with disabilities. Applying an inquiry mindset to their children who raised questions for them led to genuine and authentic inquiries that made inclusion not just a given, but something that the children themselves were invested in. The children of color with disabilities not only felt a sense of belonging; they *wanted* to remain in the classroom, engaging in all the learning experiences because they were interested in the inquiries that they pursued. For both the teachers and the students, exclusion was not an option to even consider. *Centering inquiry* was thus a DisCrit pedagogical practice that both elevated and enhanced the children's gifts as they drove their learning and made the classroom environment their own.

III

(Re)Imagining Toward DisCrit Solidarity in Inclusion Classrooms

6

Recognizing the Gifts of Resistance

IN THEIR WORK INTRODUCING the DisCrit Classroom Ecology framework, Annamma and Morrison (2018) explain that when teachers enact DisCrit Solidarity, they see behaviors that are often characterized as "challenging" as gifts of resistance. The authors specifically critique the hypersurveillance-oriented behavior management approaches that have historically been applied to children of color with disabilities. They write, "Instead of recognizing students' actions and words as responses to constraining systems, they get viewed as problematic behaviors, punished as dangerous activities, or labeled as unwanted disabilities."[1] The overemphasis on classroom or behavior management upholds hegemonic norms of behavior that are rooted in racism and ableism. A child's "goodness" is tied to how well they adhere to these norms.[2] Children of color with disabilities are then treated as though they are bad kids in need of discipline, as opposed to active resistors of inequitable systems.

Educators who are committed to DisCrit Solidarity understand that children of color with disabilities may engage in behaviors that communicate resistance and dissent against a system that aims to pathologize and exclude them for being who they are. Carla Shalaby (2017), in her book *Troublemakers*, urges readers to "think of the children who make trouble at school as miners' canaries." She goes on to write:

> I want us to imagine their behaviors—which are admittedly disruptive, hypervisible, and problematic—as both the loud sound of their suffering and a signal cry to the rest of us that there is poison in our shared air. That is, when a child is singing loudly—and sometimes more and more loudly, despite our requests for silence—we might hear that song as a signal that someone is refusing to hear her voice. And we might learn to listen, heeding her warning and searching our air for the toxin triggering her suffering, the harm that simultaneously silences her and forces her to scream out.[3]

I especially appreciate Shalaby's point that the behavior that feels challenging to adults *is* problematic. DisCrit Solidarity is not about giving children's distress a positive spin or simply allowing children to engage in behaviors that feel challenging. Enacting DisCrit Solidarity means recognizing that children behave in troubling ways because they feel they must in order to be heard. Traditional approaches to classroom management tend to focus on trying to contain the individual through behavioristic approaches. Teachers who practice DisCrit Solidarity understand that the individual's behavior is a signal that the system is not working for the child. Classrooms reproduce social inequities, and educators have the power to stand with their most distressed, multiply oppressed students in their resistance against those inequities.[4]

When children of color with disabilities resist the oppressive systems of which they are a part, they are giving educators gifts—opportunities to reflect upon and change circumstances and environments that cause harm. The children are also demonstrating capabilities that, if channeled in responsive, loving ways, can make the children of color with disabilities agents of change. As Annamma and Morrison (2018) explain,

"Using DisCrit Curriculum and Pedagogy in concert with DisCrit Solidarity productively links what students face in terms of systemic oppression with what they feel about that violence; allowing them space to own their emotions and concurrently use that passion to change the system."[5] *Recognizing the gifts of resistance*, therefore, is directly tied to the seventh tenet of DisCrit: "DisCrit requires activism and supports all forms of resistance."[6] DisCrit-aligned educators work with their children of color with disabilities to channel their resistance into activism aimed at changing the status quo.

The first step of *recognizing the gifts of resistance* is to give children space to express their emotions. Because of the bias that children of color with disabilities encounter, the automatic response to expressions of big feelings is often fear. Children of color with disabilities are seen as dangerous, defiant, and in need of control.[7] The DisCrit-aligned educators I observed responded differently. They understood that, as one teacher told me, "Kids are oppressed as soon as they're born. And school can be the place where it happens the most." Teachers who practiced DisCrit Solidarity aimed to create environments where children can express their feelings and experience healing, not control.

In her book *Emotionally Responsive Practice: A Path for Schools That Heal*, Lesley Koplow (2021) puts forth a vision for schools that "support the social and emotional infrastructure of cognitive development by appreciating and addressing the whole child's developmental issues and by communicating respect for their experiences."[8] Koplow describes educators who embrace Emotionally Responsive Practice (ERP) as "good mirrors," who respect and reflect children's experiences so they do not have to carry the burden of difficult or overwhelming experiences alone. They acknowledge the full range of affects that a child holds and expresses, be they negative or positive. While acknowledging the children's affects, ERP educators reflect a positive image back to the children. Although the DisCrit-aligned educators I observed did not all necessarily know about

ERP per se, I believe that their DisCrit Solidarity was rooted in ERP, as they made room for children's emotions to be respected and reflected in ways that facilitate healing.

The second step of *recognizing the gifts of resistance* is to channel resistance into activism. Not only are classrooms that enact DisCrit Solidarity healing spaces, they also reduce replication of trauma. Krazinski and Flores (2023) explain that for classrooms to truly heal, educators must take a proactive approach to limiting students' exposure to retraumatization.[9] This is where DisCrit Solidarity and DisCrit Pedagogy often go hand in hand. Teachers can enact pedagogical approaches that allow collective healing and solidarity across the entire classroom community. These approaches give children of color with disabilities opportunities to channel their gifts of resistance toward activism, changing the oppressive systems of which they are a part.

In the pages that follow, I share examples of good mirrors—educators who were emotionally responsive to the distress of their children of color with disabilities. These educators practiced DisCrit Solidarity by seeing their children's emotions and behaviors as gifts of resistance that needed to be respected and reflected. I then share one story from Ms. Shima and Ms. Davis's classroom, which we first encountered in chapter 3, where the educators created an opportunity for children's gifts of resistance to be acted upon in productive ways. Through these examples, I aim to paint a picture of what practicing DisCrit Solidarity with children of color with disabilities can look like.

RESPECTING AND REFLECTING BIG FEELINGS: EMOTIONALLY RESPONSIVE PRACTICE IN DISCRIT SOLIDARITY

"I can see you're feeling really mad. You're bashing that baby doll with the sheep. You are really getting your anger out." Ms. Muñoz crouches down to where Noab is standing.

Noab has a baby doll on a table and is holding it down with one hand while he hits the doll with a plastic toy sheep in his other hand. Ms. Muñoz watches as Noab continues to hit the baby doll for several minutes.

"It seems like you are really mad," Ms. Muñoz repeats. "The sheep is really slamming into that baby doll hard."

Noab exclaims, "I have to destroy it!"

"Hmmm, I'm wondering why the baby doll has to be destroyed," Ms. Muñoz replies. Noab continues to hit the doll but is slowing down. Ms. Muñoz waits and observes. Eventually, Noab stops, picks up the doll, and throws it down on the ground.

"You look mad and maybe sad," Ms. Muñoz says in a quiet voice.

Noab nods at Ms. Muñoz.

"Thank you for telling me," Ms. Muñoz says. "Do you want to talk about why you're feeling mad and sad?"

Noab shrugs.

"You know what? I see that you are really able to show your feelings, and you let out that anger in a way that didn't hurt your own body or anyone else. Thank you for that. Would it help to find a material that you can now play with without hurting it? Or would you like to go to the cozy corner to get some rest?"

Noab replies, "I want to go read a book."

"That's a really great choice," Ms. Muñoz says. "I love that you made that choice, and I know that you will be respectful with our books. But if you're feeling like you want to hit something again, come talk to me, and we'll find a way for you to do that safely."

Noab walks over to the classroom library, grabs a book, and sits on a beanbag chair with it.

In this scene in a Universal PreK inclusion classroom with Ms. Muñoz and four-year-old Noab—a Black child with an individualized education program (IEP) for Emotional Disturbance—Ms. Muñoz practices what

Koplow (2021) calls "reflective language." *Reflective language* is when an adult verbally reflects on what is happening before offering directions or asking problem-solving questions to the child. As Koplow explains, "Rather than language that reminds children to listen to the teacher or to follow rules, reflective language allows children to see and hear *themselves* during overwhelming emotional moments."[10]

Ms. Muñoz served as a good mirror to Noab by verbally stating the emotions that she was seeing him express (anger and sadness) and how she was seeing these emotions get expressed (bashing of the baby doll with a toy sheep). While reflecting on the emotions that she observed, Ms. Muñoz gave Noab the space he needed to let his feelings out. She never told him to stop bashing the doll, and when she made an "I'm wondering . . . " statement, she did not press Noab to respond. Ms. Muñoz waited for him to be finished, patiently pausing at several points or continuing to verbally reflect the feelings and behaviors she saw. When Noab finished bashing the doll, Ms. Muñoz engaged him in some problem-solving, asking if he wanted to talk or find something else to do. As Noab transitioned to the classroom library, Ms. Muñoz reminded him about the importance of keeping everyone in the classroom physically safe, while thanking him for doing so when he was expressing his anger by bashing the doll. Throughout this interaction, Ms. Muñoz reflected to Noab an image of a child who is able to communicate his feelings and is responsible with his agency around expressing those emotions.

When I observed this moment between Noab and Ms. Muñoz, I was very interested in understanding why he seemed to be angry. Ms. Muñoz, however, did not find this to be the most important element of their interaction. She said:

> I can take a guess or I could force him to tell me, but that could also cause more harm. There have been a lot of things going on at home for Noab, and then there's also just being a young Black boy with a disability in a system that's not designed for him. But if I make him talk about

all of those things, will it really make him feel better? I'm not sure. I try to follow my kids' lead.

What I took from Ms. Muñoz's response was that she wanted to give Noab room to talk about what he was feeling if he wanted to, but she was not going to force him to share. I had originally thought that understanding the "why" behind Noab's emotions might help with problem-solving and prevention of future similar episodes. Ms. Muñoz reminded me, though, that (1) forcing a child to talk about something when they are not ready can actually be retraumatizing, and (2) the important thing for Noab to know in this situation was that his feelings are welcome and he can safely express them without judgment. A classroom that heals is not one that "fixes" or eliminates big feelings. Rather, it is one that respects and reflects *all* emotions.

Respecting and reflecting all emotions do not mean that there is no room for classroom limits. In Ms. Castillo's inclusive Head Start classroom, I observed her making space for three-year-old Hector, a Latinx child with an IEP for Autism, to express his feelings physically with blocks while still maintaining norms around classroom safety:

> Hector moves quickly around the room and crashes into a magnatile tower that two of his peers are building. "Stop!" one child exclaims as he takes a magnatile and throws it at Hector. Hector makes a roaring sound in the child's face and then runs across the room to the block area. Ms. Castillo rushes over to Hector while one of her assistants checks in with the other two children over by the magnatiles. Hector picks up a block and throws it across the rug. "You're feeling angry so you threw a block," Ms. Castillo says. "It's OK to be angry," she continues, "but we don't want to hurt anyone or ourselves. You can stomp your feet." Hector begins jumping on a ramp made with a wide wooden rectangular block. He roars again. "You can scream and roar when you're angry," Ms. Castillo continues to narrate Hector's actions.

> Ms. Castillo and Hector remain in the block area for several minutes. As Hector jumps on blocks and makes roaring noises, Ms. Castillo continues to reflect his behaviors and feelings back to him: "You're angry and you're stomping your feet, jumping up and down, and shouting. It's OK to be angry." Occasionally, Hector picks up a block and throws it back onto the floor. She does not intervene and instead says, "You're throwing the block on the floor because you're angry, but you also are keeping everyone safe."
>
> Eventually, Hector stops his stomping, jumping, throwing, and roaring. He then on his own walks away from the block area and wanders over to the art table. He sits next to the teaching assistant, who helps Hector create a glittery snowflake.

In this scene, as Ms. Castillo reflected back to Hector what he was feeling and doing to express his anger, she also reminded him of the classroom norms around safety. Throwing the block in the air in a direction that could hurt another person was not safe. Ms. Castillo told Hector that "It's OK to be angry," but it was not OK for him to throw the block across the rug. When he was picking up and throwing the block on the ground, this was permissible because it was not being thrown in a direction that would harm anyone in the classroom. So long as his actions stuck to the expectations around safety, Hector could express his anger however he felt he needed to. In some ways, I think the fact that he was even given space to throw a block led him to adhere to expectations around safety. In the few instances when Hector did throw materials in a way that could cause harm, Ms. Castillo moved the rest of the children to a separate part of the room, away from the materials, and redirected Hector by giving him safer alternatives (e.g., soft blocks, beanbags, clay to throw against the wall).

Hector's moments of expressing big feelings happened throughout the school day. Ms. Castillo was often with Hector in different parts of the room, reflecting his emotions and affirming his capability to express his feelings. Each time she did this, after several minutes, Hector would stop his actions and transition to a different activity, easing his way back into the life of the classroom. The ability to safely express his emotions thus made it possible for Hector to experience belonging.

Both Ms. Muñoz and Ms. Castillo practiced DisCrit Solidarity through their emotional responsiveness. By respecting and reflecting the emotions of their children, they communicated to the children that their whole beings—inclusive of their emotional reactions to the oppressive world that they inhabited—mattered and belonged in the classroom. The teachers served as good mirrors who reflected back to Noab and Hector images of children who were capable of communicating important, valuable emotions and could do so responsibly, in ways that still cared for the community. Ms. Muñoz and Ms. Castillo understood that Noab and Hector, just by virtue of living in an ableist, racist society, experienced oppression to which they had emotional reactions. Their classrooms were ones where those emotional reactions were received and processed to allow for healing.

Like both Ms. Muñoz and Ms. Castillo, many of the DisCrit-aligned teachers I observed dedicated individualized time to their students of color with disabilities who were expressing big feelings. The teachers stopped whatever they were doing to care for the children who would benefit from ERP. In Ms. Jiménez's fifth-grade inclusion classroom, ten-year-old Justin, a multiracial child with an IEP for Other Health Impairment (ADHD) and Emotional Disturbance, was a child who often expressed feelings of sadness or anger in big, physical ways. I observed Justin throw furniture or materials, run out of the classroom, and hit and kick teachers or peers. By the middle of the school year, which is when I visited Ms. Jiménez's classroom, Ms. Jiménez and Justin had developed a system for how to approach Justin's "big feeling" moments. Ms. Jiménez would say, "Football," and she and Justin would meet in the hallway, while one of the paraprofessionals took over managing the classroom. She would bring with her a football, which she and Justin would throw back and forth to each other. Ms. Jiménez said about these ball-throwing meetings:

> At first, I had administrators coming up to me and saying, "What are you doing? You can't do that," and I just said to them, "He needs this right now." Our football-throwing in the hallway is Justin's space to decompress, let out his emotions, and tell me what's going on. I've learned that his grandfather, who he was really close to, recently passed away, and that his mom has been sick and going in and out of the hospital. I think the world feels really unfair to him right now, and being in school is not exactly easy or like where he wants to be when he's feeling that way.

Through their football-throwing sessions, Ms. Jiménez created a bit of a safe haven for Justin to get out his emotions in ways that would not harm himself or others, and also for him to share whatever he wanted to with his teacher. She saw these times as valuable opportunities for her to listen, learn, and thus respect Justin's feelings. She empathized with Justin's sense that the world was "unfair to him" and committed to giving him individualized, emotionally responsive attention because she believed that he needed it to feel more regulated in the classroom. Prioritizing time and space for teacher and child to meaningfully connect and process feelings together ultimately made Ms. Jiménez's classroom a place of greater belonging and safety for all the children.

In another DisCrit-aligned classroom that I observed, individualized time between teacher and child was used as a way to anticipate potential big feelings and retraumatization of children. Carolina was an eight-year-old third grader with an IEP for Speech or Language Impairment in Ms. Harris and Ms. Alamilla's third-grade inclusion classroom. When I visited the classroom, the children were in the process of wrapping up a unit of study on their families' immigration histories. The entire school was getting ready for a schoolwide exhibition where each classroom would essentially become a museum exhibit, displaying the learnings from the students' recent units of study. Each student, in every classroom, would have the opportunity to be a "visitor" to the classroom exhibits as well as a presenter. Here is a description of how Ms. Harris and Ms. Alamilla handled this expectation with Carolina, a student with tremendous fear of public speaking:

> The children are gathered in a clump on the rug sitting in front of Ms. Alamilla, who is explaining the exhibition process. "When it's our turn to host visitors, each of you will stand in front of your collage and will wait for visitors to come up to you," Ms. Alamilla explains. "You'll give a really short explanation of your project, which we are going to write out on note cards that you can hold and read. Then you'll answer any questions that your visitors might have."
>
> Carolina is sitting on the edge of the rug, hugging her knees into her chest and rocking back and forth. She is chewing on her lower lip, her eyes darting from side to side. Ms. Harris walks over to Carolina and sits down on the rug next to her. She puts her arm around Carolina and rocks back and forth alongside her.
>
> Ms. Alamilla then dismisses the class to line up for lunch. "Carolina, can you come meet with me?" Ms. Alamilla asks while the children walk over toward their line spots by the door. Ms. Harris goes over to the classroom door and begins monitoring the rest of the class. As the rest of the class leaves the room with Ms. Harris, Ms. Alamilla stays back to talk with Carolina. Ms. Alamilla says to Carolina, "I am thinking about what you've told me before about feeling nervous when you have to talk in front of other people." Carolina nods. "I want to make sure you know exactly what to expect on exhibition day so that you can feel confident and prepared. So let's walk through the entire day together."
>
> Ms. Alamilla proceeds to do a sort of a practice run for exhibition day with Carolina. They walk up and down the hallway so Carolina can see where all of the exhibit rooms are and can experience the path that visitors will take before they reach Ms. Harris and Ms. Alamilla's

> room. They then walk around their own classroom, and Ms. Alamilla explains where Carolina and her peers will be positioned. "You'll be standing here," Ms. Alamilla tells Carolina. "Is this an OK spot for you, or would you like to stand somewhere else?"
>
> "This is OK," Carolina responds. She and Ms. Alamilla then talk about what Carolina will say. Ms. Alamilla scribes for Carolina on a piece of paper and tells Carolina that what they worked on will be a draft of the note card that Carolina will write later that day. Ms. Alamilla encourages Carolina to read her writing a couple of times. Then they transition to lunch together.

Ms. Alamilla took this time with Carolina to give her a preview of exhibition day and a head start on figuring out what she was going to say because she knew and respected Carolina's fear of speaking in front of others. Ms. Alamilla told me during our interview, "It felt important to me that Carolina be able to participate in this celebration of her work, and I believed she could do it. She just needed some time to prepare and feel ready." She explained that she never would have forced Carolina to participate if she really did not want to do it: "That's also why I wanted to meet with her separately, though. I wanted to make sure she was OK with where she was going to stand and what she was going to say. It is always a choice, and I wanted Carolina to know that she had a choice." Ms. Alamilla, therefore, took Carolina's emotions seriously. She also, however, engaged Carolina in individualized problem solving, reflecting to Carolina an image of a child who is capable of participating in the exhibition alongside her peers should she choose to do so.

Ms. Alamilla and Ms. Harris often responded to their students' big emotions with individualized care and attention. They believed that this investment of their time was valuable in the long run. When I visited their room, I often thought, "They use the number of adults in the room so well." It was not uncommon to see one teacher providing individualized attention to a child while the other facilitated an experience with the rest of the children. Ms. Harris and Ms. Alamilla used these one-on-one interactions to slow time and make room for children to express their emotions, and for the educators to respond to them as well.

The educators described in this section all showed DisCrit Solidarity with their children of color with disabilities by respecting and reflecting the children's emotions through ERP. They thus saw their children's feelings as gifts of resistance—ways that the children were communicating their reactions to oppressive systems that aim to change them rather than honor who they are. These expressions of resistance were not to be tamped down, but rather brought to light so children could be known, seen, and valued. As the educators responded to the big feelings of their children of color with disabilities with respect, they created communities of belonging that modeled the radical care needed to combat the racism and ableism that is so deeply entrenched in our schools.

CHANNELING CHILDREN'S RESISTANCE TO DISMANTLE SYSTEMS IN DISCRIT SOLIDARITY

Once the emotions of children of color with disabilities are understood and valued, educators can begin engaging the children in transformative practice. Annamma and Handy (2019) argue that "an educator cannot simply seek to recognize emotions that multiply-marginalized students display. The educator must shift that understanding into action."[11] Along similar lines, Annamma and colleagues (2022) explain that "the power of DisCrit lies in its commitments to centering both the injustices that those from the margins experience *and* the resistance that they engage."[12] The act of (re)imagining inclusion can happen only when there are both critical analysis of unjust, pathologizing practice *and* recognition of the power to resist these practices that children of color with disabilities enact. It is in their resistance that possibilities for activism and transformation lie.

The teachers who practice DisCrit Solidarity understand that the emotions that their students of color with disabilities express stem from the oppression that the children live with daily. Seeing children of color with disabilities as human beings with tremendous gifts also means creating opportunities for them to use their gifts to practice and/or envision dismantling the systems that oppress them.[13] In other words, standing in solidarity with children of color with disabilities is about channeling their gifts of resistance to advance change.

I saw this kind of DisCrit Solidarity most tangibly in Ms. Davis and Ms. Shima's second-grade inclusion classroom. We first met Ms. Davis and Ms. Shima in chapter 3. Owen, a Black eight-year-old child with an IEP for Specific Learning Disabilities, was one of the students in their class. When I visited Ms. Davis and Ms. Shima's classroom midyear, Owen had recently moved into the area and had just started at the school a couple of months prior. According to Ms. Davis and Ms. Shima, attendance was a challenge for Owen, and he had missed many days of school since he joined their class. Perhaps because of his challenges with academic learning, he frequently asked for breaks throughout the day. While the teachers often agreed to these breaks, there were times when they set limits with Owen to ensure that he engaged with the learning content. Here is an example of how Ms. Davis approached one such interaction with Owen in an emotionally responsive way:

> The children are sitting in half-groups on opposite sides of the room, each group with a different teacher. The class is getting ready for two different read-alouds. Ms. Davis's group is about to read a book about Barack Obama. As her group gathers around her on their side of the room, Owen walks up to Ms. Davis and asks if he can take a ten-minute break. "Since we just came back from recess, I'm going to ask you to join us for this read-aloud. Then we can think about a different time when you can take your break." Ms. Davis offers Owen a couple of seating options. Owen chooses to sit on a wobble stool.
>
> As the group is reading the Barack Obama text, Owen wobbles in very large motions, almost falling off the stool a few times. At one

point, Ms. Davis pauses her reading and asks Owen, "Do you feel like you need to move? Or is this distracting?"

"No, I'm good," Owen responds. He steadies the stool some and turns his attention to Ms. Davis and the book.

As Ms. Davis reads, Owen slowly starts to wobble in big movements again. After a few minutes, he leans his body back so that he is laying on top of a chair. "Owen, are you sure you don't want to sit here?" Ms. Davis asks, pointing to a spot on the rug in front of her. Owen shakes his head no.

Ms. Davis continues to read, and Owen eventually falls onto the floor. "Hmmm. This doesn't seem to be working," Ms. Davis says to Owen. He gets up, walks over to the rug, and sits on the floor beside a peer.

At the end of the book, and after the group has engaged in a short discussion about the text, Ms. Davis sends the children off to work independently on a writing task. Owen is sitting at his desk and taps his pencil, lightly and slowly at first, but then the pace and volume increase. He then puts his head on his desk and watches as his pencil taps on the surface.

Ms. Davis walks over to Owen and asks if she can talk to him. They walk over to a corner of the room and sit across from each other. "I'm just observing something that I wanted to talk with you about. You know you're not in trouble, right?" Ms. Davis says to Owen. Owen nods his head. "I noticed that you found lots of different ways to try and stay engaged with our read aloud even though you had wanted to take a break. You were moving your body a lot on the wobble seat, maybe to help you stay focused, but then it didn't end up working out. Then I also see that you're tapping your pencil on your desk as you're thinking about what to write. Can you tell me what you're feeling?"

"I don't really like the book. It's boring. So I don't know what to write," Owen tells Ms. Davis.

"OK. Well, maybe we can find a different book to read together and talk about?" Ms. Davis asks. Owen nods. She asks him to get a book that he does feel excited about. Owen goes to his desk and brings back a Cam Jansen book. The two read it together pausing, laughing, and discussing the ideas in the book at various points. Ms. Davis then works with Owen to write a summary of what they read about. When they finish this task, Ms. Davis gives Owen the ten-minute break he had requested earlier.

This scene with Owen and Ms. Davis is emotionally responsive because of the respect and care that Ms. Davis shows Owen. She does not reprimand him about his behavior on the wobble stool. Instead, she checks in with him a couple of times about whether that still feels like a good choice and trusts him to make that choice until he falls off the stool altogether. She also checks in with him when she perceives that he is having difficulty with the writing task. When I observed this moment between Owen and Ms. Davis, I was really struck by how Ms. Davis made a point to say, "You know you're not in trouble, right?" While I am not in Owen's head, I can imagine that he might have felt nervous when his teacher asked to speak with him after he wasn't completing the task that he was assigned. Ms. Davis starting with this statement seemed to give Owen a sense of ease, allowing him to be honest with his teacher about how he felt about the work that they were doing. Ms. Davis also described her observations of Owen's behavior from a strengths-based lens. She framed his behaviors as efforts to stay engaged, thus assuming the best intent in Owen. This choice of language may have also helped to facilitate a space where he could respond to his teacher truthfully. What resulted from this interaction was a lovely moment of connection between student and teacher.

When I reflected on her interaction with Owen during our interview, Ms. Davis said:

> I think both [Ms. Shima and I] really believe in the whole-child approach. We talk about how you have to take care of yourself first. The academics feels like the easier part almost. The both of us can plan

> and figure out what to teach. But if someone's not ready emotionally or mentally, it's hard to receive any of that. So, with Owen, we've had to at times be like, OK, I'm pushing back academic expectations because there's a bigger need there. An emotional need, a social need. We have to address that first before we can do anything else.

Ms. Davis did not view Owen's behavior as acts of defiance. She saw him as communicating a need for more emotional and mental care. Krazinski and Flores (2023) say that cultivating communities of care in classrooms is part of a trauma-informed healing process that many children of color with disabilities need but do not have access to. This healing is a necessary precursor to the activist-oriented, trauma-reducing practices that the authors advocate.[14]

Aligned with the DisCrit Solidarity stance that resistance must become activism, Ms. Davis and Ms. Shima promoted activism in their own classroom through several units of study that specifically addressed social justice themes. At the time that I was observing in their classroom, the children were engaged in a unit around Black Lives Matter at School Week. The children had done research on various themes—freedom, Black families, diversity, Black women, and empathy—and were broken into small groups to create murals for each theme. When it was time for the children to start their mural project during the class's social studies block, Owen at first walked around the perimeter of the room and was drumming his hands on the shelves. The following ensued:

> "Owen, I have a job for you," Ms. Shima calls over to Owen. Owen stops his drumming and walks over to Ms. Shima, who is standing over large sheets of butcher paper that she had just rolled out onto the floor. "Can you help me make borders for our murals?" Owen nods. Ms. Shima shows him how to use a yardstick to make borders around the edges of each sheet of butcher paper. Owen gets to work immediately. He seems to take the task very seriously, working with tremendous focus and meticulousness as he draws the borders.

While Owen works, Ms. Shima and Ms. Davis give the children instructions on who is part of which group and where the groups will be positioned to work on their murals. The teachers remind the children that they are going to be drawing from the research they've done and the conversations they've had over the last several weeks about their respective topics. They also point out various resources around the room that children can use to help them as they create their murals. "You're going to have to work together to figure out what you're going to put in your murals and where you will put them," Ms. Shima explains.

When Owen is done with the borders, the teachers dismiss the various groups. All of the groups immediately jump into the task at hand, discussing with one another what they want to draw, who is going to work on what, and where the pieces they agree upon will be placed on their murals. Owen is in a group that is working on a mural about Black Families. At first, Owen stands and watches as his peers discuss their ideas for the mural and begin drawing on their butcher paper.

"Owen," one peer suddenly says as he turns to Owen, "What do you want to add?"

Owen walks closer to the mural and looks down on the paper that his peers have begun to work on. "You see how it says 'forever'?" Owen says, pointing to a word written on the top-right corner of the mural. "What if I wrote 'together' so it's 'forever together'?"

"That's a great idea!" another peer says, as she hands Owen a pencil. Owen begins to write "together" on the mural. He then continues to offer suggestions for what he can draw and work on.

The mural project described here is one of many examples of how Ms. Shima and Ms. Davis took an activist-oriented stance in their classroom. They understood that, as Ms. Shima said, "the kids live in a biased system" that especially affects their children of color with disabilities. It was important to the teachers that their students knew that they had agency to change the troubling, biased systems of oppression in which they lived. Ms. Shima and Ms. Davis shared with me that the class had voted on which of the Black Lives Matter principles they wanted to focus on in their unit of study. They thus had much decision-making power in their learning around this social justice topic.

The mural project seemed to be a powerful way for Owen to channel his gifts. As evident in the example with the read-aloud described earlier, Owen was a child who had strong ideas and preferences, as well as the capability to express those ideas and preferences in a variety of ways. He was able to apply his strong ideas and communication skills to his group's collaborative mural development. He also showed himself to be a child with good follow-through and execution when motivated by a task, as evident in both his meticulous border-making and his contributions to his group's mural.

Owen is just one of several children of color with disabilities who benefited from the DisCrit Solidarity that Ms. Shima and Ms. Davis showed their children. By creating an environment where children's emotional responses to the oppressive world in which they lived were seen, respected, and reflected, the teachers communicated to their students that their whole beings mattered. They then provided opportunities for their students to reimagine the world around them, engaging in long-term projects around a range of social justice topics. In so doing, they simultaneously *taught about* dismantling systems and *enacted* a dismantling of oppressive systems themselves. Owen's experience in his second-grade classroom countered the traditional exclusionary approaches that children like him are often subjected to in schools around the country. Instead of punishing him, Ms. Shima and Ms. Davis gave him agency to be his full self and to envision a world where systems of oppression do not predominate. The mural project was the time when I saw Owen be most engaged. His gifts were channeled productively when he could take this activist stance, and he did so collectively with his peers. True DisCrit Solidarity occurs when healing can become a collective endeavor, as it did in Ms. Shima and Ms. Davis's classroom.[15]

As shown in this chapter, fully recognizing the gifts of resistance involves a two-step process. It requires first respecting and reflecting the big emotions that children of color with disabilities have in reaction to the systems of oppression they endure. ERP offers a framework for approaching children's feelings and expressions of those feelings with care. Emotionally responsive teachers serve as good mirrors to children of color with disabilities, who reflect an image of children full of gifts. Once these gifts are recognized, teachers who enact DisCrit Solidarity create opportunities for children to channel those gifts into activist-oriented experiences that move to dismantle oppressive systems. Although these opportunities can be individual in nature, the most impactful DisCrit Solidarity happens when collective resistance is embraced. It is when children of color with disabilities can collectively act upon their emotional responses to the ableist, racist systems that they endure that they feel a strong sense of purpose and engage in genuine trauma-informed resistance.

7

Centering Relationships

FOR ALL THE DISCRIT-ALIGNED teachers I observed, solidarity with their children of color with disabilities was possible because they *centered relationships*. As Annamma and Handy (2019) explain, "Using a DisCrit lens requires us to centre relationships because it requires a change in how educators imagine disabled students of colour in their classrooms."[1] *Centering relationships* means seeing children of color with disabilities as whole human beings. It means getting to know children—their strengths, interests, and stressors—and wanting them to be their full selves in the classroom, accepting all the parts of themselves that they bring with them. It means valuing children and seeking to understand them, especially when doing so feels hard. DisCrit teachers who center relationships do not blame, shame, or exclude children of color with disabilities. Their primary aim is belonging. These teachers strive to ensure that their students of color with disabilities know that they are valued members of the community.

I believe that to center relationships with their students of color with disabilities, the DisCrit-aligned teachers practice a radical kind of love, like the kind that bell hooks writes about in her 2001 book, *All about Love: New Visions*. She teaches us, "To truly love we must learn to mix various ingredients—care, affection, recognition, respect, commitment, and trust, as well as honest and open communication."[2] Further, hooks does not put conditions on these ingredients. A loving teacher practices all these acts with children, even when they experience pain, anger, or fear. She says, "When we face pain in relationships our first response is often to sever bonds rather than to maintain commitment."[3] Children's acts of resistance can feel painful. Before they feel a sense of reciprocal trust with their educators, children of color with disabilities might see their teachers as authority figures whose job it is to uphold the oppressive systems that the children are trying to resist. Teachers who "truly love" stay committed to their students in these moments of pain, seeking repair rather than separation.

Migliarini and Annamma (2019) expand on hooks's idea that to truly love requires care. They explain that to practice DisCrit Solidarity, teachers must embrace authentic care: care that is rooted in an understanding of power differences and systemic oppression.[4] When DisCrit-aligned teachers commit to building reciprocal, trusting relationships with children of color with disabilities, the teachers acknowledge that they hold a lot of power. This power can be used to perpetuate the oppression that the children resist, or it can be used to resist alongside children. Educators who authentically care welcome student resistance, responding with a desire to listen and understand, not to control. When educators can understand what their children of color with disabilities are communicating through their acts of resistance, teachers are able to see children more fully, engage in honest and open communication, and build trust.

In what follows, I'd like to revisit three educators whom we met previously: Ms. Gallagher, Ms. Allen, and Ms. Reyes. In their interviews, these educators detailed what it means to "truly love," in the way that hooks defines this act. Analyzing their perspectives helps us better understand how to *center relationships* that are rooted in love with children of color with disabilities. I will then share one final story of the transformative power of relationships. The stories of the educators described in this chapter show us how *centering relationships* is a DisCrit Solidarity move that must serve as the foundation for all other DisCrit Pedagogy and Solidarity practices to take place.

IN THEIR WORDS: DISCRIT-ALIGNED TEACHERS' DESCRIPTIONS OF *CENTERING RELATIONSHIPS*

In all my interviews with the DisCrit-aligned educators, I asked them to reflect on their work with their children of color with disabilities. Ms. Gallagher—whom we met in chapter 4—spoke about her work with five-year-old Loretta in a way that exemplified bell hooks's definition of loving truly. As we learned in chapter 4, Loretta initially had difficulty feeling comfortable in her kindergarten classroom. It took several months for the teachers to establish trust with her so she would not run out of the classroom every day. They invested heavily in building relationships centered on authentic care with her.

This process of relationship-building was not without its challenges. Loretta sometimes moved her body in ways that could cause physical pain to the adults working with her. In many school settings, these painful experiences would lead educators to push children of color with disabilities like Loretta out of their classrooms. This was not the case for Loretta's teachers, though. Ms. Gallagher told me:

> She doesn't understand her own strength. Once she was sitting criss-cross applesauce in my lap. Something got her very excited, and she ended up head-butting me in the nose. I almost thought I was gonna pass out. I had to leave and go to the nurse and get an ice pack and let my body deal with the impact of this blow on the nose. And one time before that, she had slammed her body into my left shoulder. Of course, it's the shoulder where I have an injury. It wasn't my right

> shoulder, which is good. It was my left. That also just kind of caught me off guard. I just didn't quite know how to respond. We were all very conscious that that could happen at any second, and it was hard to anticipate. We really couldn't anticipate it at the beginning until we got to know her better. Just very quick, strong movements. She wasn't trying to hurt anybody. It was very clear that it wasn't intentional. She just had a really hard time expressing her feelings, regulating her body. She just didn't have the language or the skills yet to show excitement in a way that was safe to everybody.

The teachers working with Loretta remained committed to her even when they feared being physically hurt. My favorite part of the quote from Ms. Gallagher is when she says, "We really couldn't anticipate it at the beginning *until we got to know her better.*" For Loretta's teachers, severing their bond with Loretta in response to their experience of pain was not an option. Instead, they were committed to getting to know Loretta better—not so they could change her, but so they could read her cues and figure out how to manage their own reactions when she had those moments of moving her body in big, sudden ways.

Ms. Gallagher was able to have this relational approach to Loretta because of her own personal experiences with trauma. Loretta's physical behaviors triggered for Ms. Gallagher traumatic memories from her own life. Ms. Gallagher spoke about how well-meaning adults who don't want to be angry with children could get mad if their past traumas are triggered by students' behavior. As she said to me, "It's hard because it brings up your own stuff. But then, well, this is why this work is so important." She felt that because she knew what it was like to have her trauma triggered, she was able to have greater compassion toward Loretta. She understood that there were traumas that were triggered for Loretta in school.

Ms. Gallagher's way of thinking about Loretta and trauma was surprising to me at first. In many other instances, if a child triggers trauma in a teacher, the teacher often responds with anger, hurt, and a desire to sever bonds. In other words, triggered trauma leads to a fight, flight, or freeze response from the adult toward the child. For Ms. Gallagher, however, when Loretta triggered her trauma, she was able to step back and see how Loretta might also be acting from a place of triggered trauma. Ms. Gallagher explained:

> We all kind of understood that there was some kind of trauma. And it reinforced for us why we wanted to invest in this relationship. Because if you've been there, then you know how awful it is. You also know how easily triggered it is. So, it made me kind of more committed to relationship with Loretta . . . I ended up having the resources I need. But, when she leaves schools, who knows what kind of resources she'll have? It's also just so important to do that kind of relationship-building, coping work when they're that young, because that's when who they are going to be becomes, not set completely, but a huge indicator of how they're going to cope with later stresses in life or later trauma.

For Ms. Gallagher, the old adage "Hurt people hurt people" became "Hurt people *understand and love* hurt people." Her commitment to building relationship with Loretta was rooted in her sense of responsibility to ensure that Loretta was able to experience healing and develop healthy coping mechanisms for any additional stressors or trauma she might encounter. Her response to experiences of pain and triggered trauma with Loretta was not the severing of relationship, but a deeper leaning into it. She *centered relationship* with Loretta because she had compassion, genuinely cared, and understood that Loretta would be spending the rest of her life in a world full of pain and harm. Ms. Gallagher's self-reflectiveness, her critical thinking about injustice, and her commitment to young children's care made her *center relationship* with Loretta.

In her book, bell hooks writes, "Profound changes in the way we think and act must take place if we are to create a loving culture."[5] The kind of love that Loretta's teachers showed her was radically different from what so many children of color with disabilities experience in schools. Ms. Gallagher and her colleagues *centered relationship* by responding to Loretta with a desire to understand and offer healing, rather than trying to control and contain her. In our interview, Ms. Gallagher reflected on the first time that Loretta ever ran away from the class:

> We were walking outside for snack time when she made a run for it. Mr. Taylor followed her, but she was really upset, so not only was she running, she needed somebody to comfort her. Mr. Taylor is like six-foot four, and he's a big teddy bear. He's got an incredible, gentle way with kids. I'll never forget the way he picked her up like she was a feather and wrapped his arms around her. He held her and hugged her and let her cry it all out. That's how you know things are different in our classroom.

Here, we see that hooks's ingredients of "care, affection, recognition, respect, commitment, and trust, as well as honest and open communication" were fully present in the relationship-building that took place between Loretta and her teachers.[6] The teachers saw Loretta as a child to "truly love," not punish. *Centering relationship* with Loretta involved recognizing that her behaviors were a response to the injustices that she had already encountered at such a young age. The teachers understood that to be in a truly loving relationship with Loretta, they needed to interact with her in ways that allowed healing rather than discipline or exclusion.

Ms. Allen, whom we met in chapter 3, similarly responded to children's behaviors with a desire to understand and ensure repair. Her respect for and trust of her students was at the heart of how she *centered relationships.* During one of our interviews, Ms. Allen shared that her biggest worry about the field of education is "kids not getting a voice." She spoke about how many teachers will get into power struggles with children of color with disabilities, which lead to punishment rather than listening and mutual care. As she put it:

> Often, they have a valid reason for being this negative toward what you're asking them to do or telling them to do. And sometimes the tone that you use too, you're not being kind, so they're not going to be kind to you either. You're not being respectful, so they're not going to be respectful to you either.

Ms. Allen went on to share the following story about a Black student with an individualized education program (IEP), whom she used to teach in her kindergarten classroom:

> When he went to third grade, he tortured that teacher. That's the only thing I could say to you. That's the word to use. One day, I asked him why. And he said, "I don't like her. She doesn't let me talk. She doesn't let me explain anything. She's always blaming me for everything. So I don't like her. And I'm not going to be nice to her." Oh, Lord. She wasn't a teacher that I could go and talk to her about this. The best I could do was just ask him to be a little kinder, you know? Because he was being really rude to her. I was like, "What is going on? Why are you doing this?" And he's a kid that likes to talk. We had conversations. That's how I used to get through to him when he was available. We'd have conversations and we'd have a back-and-forth thing. "OK, so what do you think?" And then we'd come to a conclusion, and it was fine. But she wasn't giving him that space. So, he decided, "Well fine, then you're gonna get the worst of me."

In this story, Ms. Allen emphasizes the importance of respect, trust, and honest and open communication—three of the ingredients for true love in bell hooks's work. When Ms. Allen worked with the child she describes, she engaged in open conversations with him about his behavior because she *centered relationship*. Being in a two-way relationship with another person requires respect and kindness, which the child's third-grade teacher was unwilling to show him. When the child was in Ms. Allen's kindergarten classroom, Ms. Allen wanted to understand the "why" behind his behaviors so she could partner with him to come up with solutions together. The child's third-grade teacher did not demonstrate the same kind of curiosity, desire to understand, and trust in the child as Ms. Allen did. According to the child, the third-grade teacher made assumptions about him and blamed him without giving him an opportunity to explain.

Ms. Allen continued by further describing her worry that children of color with disabilities don't have a voice in school:

> My worry is kids not getting the chance to be who they are. To voice their opinion. To say, "I don't want to sit here." Something as simple as where you sit on the rug, or how you sit, or do you even want to sit on the rug. That shouldn't be something that you argue with a kid over, you know? There's been many students I had, who they can't sit still. They just cannot. OK, so you sit on the edges where you can rock all you want and not trample everybody. Or there's a chair. The chairs are close to wherever there's a desk. A chair that's close to the rug. Choose that. Give them the other options that you have. "OK, you can't do this or for whatever reason you won't do this. Then here are your other options." Don't just be so rigid, "You have to do what I tell you to do, because I tell you to do this."

From Ms. Allen's perspective, the many power struggles that teachers and children got into often stemmed from teachers being too rigid. There are many ways that children are silenced. If they are simply listened to and given a "chance to be who they are," there are often simple solutions that teachers can find. In how Ms. Allen and Ms. Campbell related to their students in chapter 3, we saw that making room for children to voice their opinions, share their thinking, and express their feelings fostered a respectful, loving community where everyone belonged. In Ms. Allen's view, *centering relationships* required the simple act of listening and having honest, open communication with children so they could be their full selves.

This theme of *centering relationships* so that children can "be who they are" was also a driving force in Ms. Reyes's practice. Ms. Reyes, whom we met in chapter 5, thought about communication in an expansive way to ensure that she was really listening to children and understanding their intent. Some of the children of color with disabilities in her classroom did not use verbal language to communicate. Ms. Reyes felt that it was important to listen to children regardless of their mode of communication. As she explained, "Children are communicating something, whether they have words or not. Language doesn't always have to be words." She went on to tell me how this standpoint allowed her to respond to children of color with disabilities with love and care:

> Just knowing that really opened a doorway for me to say, "OK, how am I going to have this child a part of my classroom community?" He can't tell me what he wants, but he is telling me his needs. If he's flailing his arms, if he's throwing himself on the floor, and if I see he's spiraling in emotional outbursts, he's trying to tell me something, you know? It's the same thing with my son's child. When he starts having these really intense moments, I know he's thirsty, and I get water. I say, "OK, come on, let's drink water." And he starts hydrating himself because he can't say, "I'm thirsty." He can't say, "I'm hungry." I can't leave him there all day and say, "Oh well, he's having a fit. I'm just gonna leave him there. And we'll just continue on our day." I can't do that. It's not fair for them because they're trying to communicate something. So now we know when he starts having those moments, we run, we get him water. And not only have we learned that that's his way of saying, "I'm thirsty," but he now knows how to drink from an open container. He knows how to drink from a straw. So we're building his life skills as well.

Here, Ms. Reyes conveys how *centering relationship* for her is about seeing all children's behavior as a form of communication, and then working to understand what is being communicated. Listening to the communications of children of color with disabilities in their various forms is essential to being able to meet the children's needs. As she showed in her example of her grandson, when Ms. Reyes sought to listen, understand, and respond to children's communication, she was also able to support them in their growth and development. Ms. Reyes's expansive view of language stemmed from her desire to *center relationship* because she knew that doing so was at the heart of supporting children to be their full selves.

Ms. Gallagher, Ms. Allen, and Ms. Reyes help us to see that *centering relationship* with children of color with disabilities occurs when teachers see children's behaviors as responses to systemic injustices and the traumas that these injustices cause, when they create space for open and honest communication with children, when they let go of their rigid ideas and prioritize letting children "be who they are," and when they have expansive ideas about what children's being and communicating can entail. In all cases, the teachers value, listen to, and seek to understand their students of color with disabilities. The DisCrit Solidarity practice of *centering relationships* is what lays the foundation for educators to *respond with respect not restriction, make room for the unexpected, center inquiry,* and *recognize the gifts of resistance.* (Re)Imagining inclusion for children of color with disabilities thus requires *centering relationships* so the children can experience true love and belonging.

THE TRANSFORMATIVE POWER OF CENTERING RELATIONSHIPS: THE CASE OF ALEXIS

When I first met veteran educator Ms. De Waal, she told me that she had one student who was making her experience as a teacher "very challenging." "In my twenty-five years of teaching," she said, "I have never felt so burnt out and exhausted." Six-year-old Alexis was a Black girl with an IEP for Other Health Impairment (she was considered a medically fragile child with a number of health conditions) in Ms. De Waal's inclusion classroom of twenty-two first graders. The school that Alexis attended was predominantly Black and Latinx, and a majority of the students qualified for free and reduced-price lunch. Ms. De Waal did not know much about Alexis's background. She did know that she lived alone with her mother, although she and her mother lived close to a large network of extended family members who supported them. Ms. De Waal described Alexis as a "spunky, expressive child who can communicate her feelings with ease," but "when she feels tired—which is often, due to her conditions—she has a hard time following directions." Ms. De Waal went on:

> Each day is different from the next, and it can be difficult to predict how the day will progress until she enters the classroom each morning. Alexis has really extreme behaviors. I think she is seeking attention, positive or negative. She often has extreme reactions to minor incidents or circumstances. She doesn't have the cognitive capability to tell us exactly what's going on for her. So, her behavior is speaking for whatever pain she's experiencing emotionally. She genuinely likes the other kids in the class, but she doesn't observe physical boundaries and doesn't really use age-appropriate language. So it's hard for others to connect. She is also absent at least once a week because of her health challenges. I am genuinely concerned about her ability to attend and complete classwork. She has difficulty staying on task regardless of the subject. I am also concerned about how well she retains information from one day to the next.

When I asked Ms. De Waal to elaborate on what she meant by "extreme behaviors," she shared, "Alexis will suddenly run up to you and give you a tight hug if she's feeling happy. But then in the next minute, she'll be hitting the same exact person in rage. She's especially impulsive when she's upset. It's not unusual for her to spit, bite, or throw herself on the floor."

During one of my visits to Ms. De Waal's first-grade classroom, I heard a child screaming in the hallway as I approached the room. Alexis was on the floor, holding onto the legs of a table, screaming, crying, and kicking an adult who was talking to her. The adult seemed to have a behavior chart of sorts by her side and was attempting to calm Alexis down using the chart. When I walked into the classroom, Ms. De Waal told me that another child teased Alexis for something she was wearing. "It just totally set her off. She turned around, slapped the other child in the face, and began taking things off the shelves and tables and throwing them. One of our behavior specialists had to come and carry her out of the room." Later that day, Ms. De Waal told me that she was feeling extremely exhausted and unsupported. She was contemplating leaving the school altogether because "every day is just so unpredictable. I go home and I immediately crash."

After several visits to Ms. De Waal's classroom, I felt concerned about both the sheer number of times that Alexis was removed from the classroom and Ms. De Waal's emotional and physical well-being. It seemed clear that something needed to change before Alexis and/or Ms. De Waal were entirely pushed out of the classroom or school. One day, Ms. De Waal asked if we could speak over the phone after school. She said that she wanted to speak with me as someone who works in teacher education and understands the field more broadly. During our call, Ms. De Waal told me that she was seriously thinking about leaving her job. She sought my recommendations for how to proceed, and she also asked if I could help connect her with any job openings that I knew of. In my role as a researcher, I typically did not give teachers advice, as I did not see that as my place. My goal was to learn from them and their practices. Ms. De Waal was quite emotional in our conversation, however, and requested my insights.

I told Ms. De Waal that I wondered if she might set aside time each day or each week to connect with Alexis individually and build a relationship with her. I shared that it seemed like Alexis needed to have someone in the room with whom she could deeply connect and in whom she could confide when she was experiencing intense emotions. It also seemed like Ms. De Waal would benefit from finding ways to enjoy Alexis more. I told Ms. De Waal about my own experiences working with children who pushed my limits in ways that felt hard. Getting to know the children and developing relationships with them sometimes made all the difference. We also talked about how, even with other adults, prioritizing connection and relationship-building are often effective ways to move toward healing and reconciliation when we experience conflict.

Ms. De Waal decided to try establishing a weekly time when she and Alexis would work together on two activities that they both enjoyed: art and dance. Every week, the children went to the school library for a specials class. This was a period where it was difficult for Alexis to remain engaged. She had run away from the library a few times throughout the year. The librarian asked that a teacher stay with Alexis during that period; Ms. De Waal agreed to do so, and therefore she had already given up that prep time. She spoke with the librarian about working separately, one on one, with Alexis during the library period. The librarian agreed. Ms. De Waal wanted to make Alexis feel like it was a special time for the two of them, so she coordinated with her administrators to use a separate, unused room for their one-on-one work. "I didn't want Alexis to feel like she was being kept in the classroom when the rest of her class got to leave, as if she were in trouble. And I also thought she might like having a separate sacred kind of space for our work together," she told me.

Their sessions began with Ms. De Waal asking Alexis about her interests. "I know from talking with Alexis's mom that they watch a lot of movies together," she explained in an interview. "In our first session, we talked a lot about *Frozen* and *Frozen II* in particular. So then in our second session, we made snowflakes and then choreographed a dance to 'Let it Go.'" This process of coming up with dance moves to different songs became a central component of Ms. De Waal and Alexis's sessions. Ms. De Waal was formerly a dancer, so she enjoyed getting to share her passion with Alexis. Alexis in turn got to learn more about dance terminology and had a creative outlet to move her body in big ways. "I think it kind of grounds her and helps her stay more centered in the classroom too. Sometimes in the classroom, she'll dance as an expression of some of her big feelings—positive or negative—and so this kind of lets her get all of those feelings out," Ms. De Waal reflected.

For National Poetry Month in April, each class in the school was to memorize a different poem to recite. The classes were then to perform their poems at the schoolwide assembly at the end of the month. Ms. De Waal thought that this could be a good opportunity to give Alexis a leadership role in the class. In their weekly sessions, the two of them worked on movements to go along with the poem that their class was assigned. Alexis was then responsible for teaching the class the movements that they came up with. "It was very sweet. She wanted me to record her leading the class because she wanted to show her mom," Ms. De Waal recalled. "It was just so wonderful seeing her stand up at the front of the room and look so confident. I thought, 'Wow, she has really transformed.' She never would have done this a few months ago." She showed me the video of Alexis teaching her class the movements for the poem. I, too, was struck by Alexis's confident air and seeming glow around her. She had a giant grin on her face as she demonstrated each movement with big gestures. At the end, Alexis took a bow while her classmates applauded her. The pride in her expression was palpable.

By *centering relationship* with Alexis, Ms. De Waal was able to experience a side of Alexis that she did not know existed: a natural, creative leader who enjoys sharing her talent and expertise with others. Before they began the weekly sessions, Ms. De Waal's perspective of Alexis was utterly clouded by the emotional drain that she felt after experiencing many challenging moments with Alexis. Through their one-on-one time with each other, Ms. De Waal was able to take joy in Alexis. The tension that she felt began to ease, and she found new purpose in her work. This made both Alexis and Ms. De Waal more likely to stay in their collective classroom. As Ms. De Waal reflected on her journey with Alexis, she shared the following thoughts:

> Across our year together, Alexis has often puzzled me, but she also continues to surprise and teach me every day. I didn't think it was possible, but somehow, I have been able to create a significant bond with an extraordinary child, and through our relationship, I've come to see her many positive attributes. I've also seen over time my own emotional growth. Turns out I am really good at being present with a child, no matter how challenging the circumstances! I feel certain that I have been able to help Alexis's self-confidence grow as she learned to center herself and have opportunities to lead others.

Centering relationships allowed Ms. De Waal to see Alexis and herself in new ways. When she felt completely stuck and unsure of her own capacity to continue teaching in her classroom, it was prioritizing connection with the child who challenged her most that re-invigorated Ms. De Waal. Alexis also was able to shine in ways that she had not before. Although she did continue to have "big feeling" moments that involved large physical movements, the frequency significantly decreased. This was in part because she started making more friends in the classroom. It was as if developing a stronger relationship with Ms. De Waal gave Alexis the ability to make stronger relationships with her peers as well. Her opportunities to lead the group in their poetry movements changed her status in the classroom, as she was viewed by all as a capable, talented leader. *Centering relationships* ultimately made it possible for Alexis to feel a sense of belonging in her first-grade classroom.

At the end of her chapter titled "Healing: Redemptive Love," bell hooks (2001) writes the following:

> When we love, we no longer allow our hearts to be held captive by fear. Power gives us the illusion of having triumphed over fear, over our need for love. To return to love, to know perfect love, we surrender the will to power. It is this revelation that makes the scriptures on perfect love so prophetic and revolutionary for our times. We cannot know love if we remain unable to surrender our attachment to power.[7]

All the DisCrit-aligned teachers who *centered relationships* with their children of color with disabilities were able to truly love their children because they "surrender[ed their] attachment to power." They did not see it as their job to control or change their children of color with disabilities. Instead of control, they chose connection. Instead of fear, they chose curiosity and understanding. Instead of power, they chose love. Their desire to know, and truly love, their children of color with disabilities ultimately opened the door to additional DisCrit Pedagogy and Solidarity moves that fostered genuine inclusion. It was through relationship that healing and transformation were possible—for both children and teachers.

Conclusion

IN THE INTRODUCTION TO their book *DisCrit Expanded: Reverberations, Ruptures, and Inquiries,* Annamma, Ferri, and Connor (2022) write, "The goal of DisCrit is to create a theory that is responsive to the immense inequities occurring in daily life."[1] The theory they coined was, therefore, never meant to remain just an idea. DisCrit was developed to inspire action—action against the systemic injustices that children of color with disabilities experience in schools every day. The descriptions of the educators' practices provided in this book offer a concrete operationalization of such DisCrit-aligned action. The teachers countered the prevailing exclusion, isolation, and segregation of children of color with disabilities by cultivating classrooms of belonging. They did this through the DisCrit Pedagogy moves of *responding with respect not restriction, making room for the unexpected,* and *centering inquiry.* These DisCrit Pedagogy practices were made possible because the educators practiced DisCrit Solidarity by *recognizing the gifts of resistance* and *centering relationship.*

The teachers featured in this book provide us with evidence that the exclusion of children of color with disabilities does not need to be the status quo. We can (re)imagine inclusion classrooms to be spaces of belonging for children of color with disabilities, where their many gifts are seen, valued, and built upon. In such classrooms, children of color with disabilities are not viewed as problems to be fixed, as they would be in medical model–aligned classrooms.[2] Instead, they are seen as important agents of resistance against the racist, ableist, and linguicist injustices that they encounter in schools daily. Children of color with disabilities are thus viewed and interacted with as powerful human beings who not only belong with nondisabled peers, but who must be understood meaningfully for radical transformation of schooling to take place.

While the radical transformation that I call for here does aim to eliminate exclusion for children of color with disabilities, I also believe that the DisCrit practices detailed in this book put forth an entirely new culture of schooling—one that is centered on belonging for *all* and rejects the dominant culture of white, Eurocentric, middle-class, nondisabled, English-speaking, and capitalistic norms that currently predominate in US schools. The DisCrit-aligned teachers did not enact their DisCrit Pedagogy and DisCrit Solidarity approaches solely to ensure inclusion for their children of color with disabilities, although they did do so successfully. The teachers were motivated by a fundamental belief that all their children—regardless of race, ability, class, temperament, nationality, or other characteristics—were worthy of love, respect, care, and belonging. Efficiency, competition, labeling, and pathologization were all tossed to the side as the humanity of each child was honored.

The DisCrit practices detailed in this book offer several important implications for inclusive practice, policy, and research. As I bring this discussion to a close, I offer some reflections on the conclusions that we can draw from the stories told in this book. The approaches described in sections II and III lay the groundwork for what Bettina Love (2019) calls "freedom dreaming . . . dreams grounded in a critique of injustice" that are "not whimsical, unattainable daydreams [but] critical and imaginative dreams of collective resistance."[3] Love goes on to say:

> Freedom dreaming is imagining worlds that are just, representing people's full humanity, centering people left on the edges, thriving

> in solidary with folx from different identities who have struggled together for justice, and knowing that dreams are just around the corner with the might of people power.[4]

Love explains that freedom dreaming is necessary to move toward more liberatory educational practice and systems because our status quo has become "so rationalized and normalized."[5] What we need is a new vision—a new way of seeing what is possible for children of color with disabilities and the educators who work with them. This new vision must exist at the level of both classroom practice and systemic change for true transformation to take place. The DisCrit-aligned educators and children of color with disabilities featured in this book help us to see what is needed in educational practice and policy to (re)imagine inclusion so that schooling will truly honor the full humanity of children of color with disabilities.

WHAT EDUCATORS NEED TO (RE)IMAGINE INCLUSION

The implications for educational practice may seem rather obvious. All educators need to do is adopt the DisCrit Pedagogy and DisCrit Solidarity approaches described in this book, right? It is no small feat to learn to *respond with respect not restriction, make room for the unexpected, center inquiry, recognize the gifts of resistance,* or *center relationship,* especially when a child is behaving in ways that feel challenging. Teachers report that what they deem to be "challenging behavior" is a strong factor in recent high rates of burnout and turnover.[6] As Ms. Gallagher reminded us in chapter 7, "It's hard because it brings up your own stuff." Educators are human beings, with their own set of limits, histories, experiences, and dispositions. Asking someone whose lid has flipped and who is operating from fight, flight, or freeze mode to *respond with respect not restriction* is not exactly respectful to the individual and their own personhood. Telling a teacher who has never experienced, let alone planned for, inquiry-based learning to *center inquiry*, particularly when they are already having difficulty planning and implementing lessons that are accessible to all their students, is discouraging.

For educators to be able to adopt the DisCrit Pedagogy and DisCrit Solidarity practices described in this book, we must reimagine inclusive teacher preparation and professional development. DisCrit-oriented teacher preparation and professional development would include the following components:

- Shifting teachers' ways of seeing children of color with disabilities away from deficit-based lenses to assets-based ones
- Learning to value rather than change children of color with disabilities
- Unlearning normative expectations often held in school
- Engaging in critical analysis of educational—specifically special education—systems that serve to oppress children of color with disabilities, particularly interrogating the interlocking oppressions of racism and ableism at work in schools
- Critiquing traditional approaches to behavior and classroom management
- Developing their own stance on and approaches to DisCrit Pedagogy and DisCrit Solidarity

Next, I describe in further detail what teacher preparation and professional development might entail to advance belonging and inclusion for children of color with disabilities.

Changing Teachers' Way of Seeing and Responding

For educators to enact the kind of DisCrit Pedagogy and DisCrit Solidarity described in this book, they must learn to see and respond to their children of color with disabilities from an assets-based lens, recognizing their many gifts and finding ways for these gifts to shine. When I think about the differences between the medical model–aligned educators described in chapter 1 and the DisCrit-aligned educators in chapters 3–7, the first distinction that I see is the difference in how the educators see themselves relative to their children of color with disabilities.

When educators view their children of color with disabilities as "problems to be fixed," they position themselves as powerful beings who can mold the children into an "ideal child" that is rooted in white, nondisabled, middle-class, Standard English–speaking norms. The educators then use extreme, restrictive, and isolating approaches to subject children of color with disabilities to conformity; and when the children do not comply, they are pushed out of the classroom or school. In contrast, DisCrit-aligned educators do not see themselves as the all-powerful, all-knowing sage in the classroom, whose job it is to turn their students into docile, obedient citizens. DisCrit educators position themselves as learners alongside the children because they recognize that children of color with disabilities bring valuable gifts with them into the classroom. These educators see it as their primary responsibility to support the children to be their full selves. They are not interested in changing children. Instead, they strive to change the circumstances surrounding their children of color with disabilities that cause them harm.

The DisCrit-aligned educators in this book were able to enact DisCrit Pedagogy and DisCrit Solidarity practices with children of color with disabilities because they loved and valued the children just as they were. They did not have in mind a particular way of being that their children of color with disabilities must fit. The educators began with curiosity to understand, not conformity to norms. As one teacher put it, "I just let them be." In this way, the educators adhere to Annamma and colleagues' (2013) point—namely, that "DisCrit recognizes that normative cultural standards such as whiteness and ability lead to viewing differences among certain individuals as deficits."[7] To be a DisCrit-aligned, inclusive educator, therefore, involves removing from one's mind any normative expectations around how children should behave in the classroom. The

DisCrit-aligned inclusive educator understands that holding children to white, nondisabled, middle-class standards leads to the exclusion of children of color with disabilities. To ensure belonging for all students means learning to see, value, and love children for who they are.

Critical Analysis of Existing Educational Systems and Culture

Teacher preparation and professional development that is committed to promoting true belonging for children of color with disabilities will encourage educators to see both the schooling system and individual children of color with disabilities from a DisCrit lens. This simultaneous critical analysis of structural systems and interpersonal relationships might begin with the troubling of traditional behavior management beliefs and approaches. Migliarini and Annamma (2019) make a case for teacher preparation programs to incorporate coursework in which educators learn about the historic, sociopolitical implications of behavioristic approaches to classroom management that emphasize controlling "undesired" behavior and rewarding "good" behavior. The educators discuss how these approaches reproduce racism and ableism in schools.

Migliarini and Annamma (2019) explain that in this course, "we emphasize the various forms of oppression that impact on the daily lives of multiply marginalized students of color, and consequently affect their behavior, and how they navigate educational and social institutions with savvy and ingenuity."[8] The authors argue that if educators learn that children of color with disabilities are deeply affected by the interdependent and invisible ways that racism and ableism are at work in schools, they will shift their mindsets "from managing behaviors to building solidarity with multiply marginalized students of color."[9] This type of reframing serves as a critical starting point for teacher education and professional development aimed at advancing social justice for children of color with disabilities.

Developing One's Own DisCrit Pedagogy and DisCrit Solidarity Approach

Once the educators have a strong understanding of why traditional approaches to classroom and behavior management are harmful to children of color with disabilities, they will develop alternative ways of interacting with their children. They can learn about the DisCrit Solidarity and DisCrit Pedagogy moves presented in this book and also develop their own philosophies for relationship building and cultivating just, equitable classroom environments for children of color with disabilities. While I strongly believe that the practices in this book can help to reimagine inclusive classrooms as spaces of genuine belonging for children of color with disabilities, I also know that each individual educator must develop his or her own style and philosophy that feels authentic. The practices described in this book, therefore, are not meant to be prescriptive, but rather a starting point for educators to engage in their own, individual (re)imagining that is rooted in a commitment to true inclusion and an elimination of the exclusionary practices that are so pervasive in schools.

Through this process of (re)imagining what schooling is and what it could be for children of color with disabilities, educators will come to see themselves in a different light. Taking a more humanizing, DisCrit-oriented stance toward working with children of color with disabilities might challenge educators' sense of calling to the field of education, or special education more specifically. Thorius (2016) found that special education teachers often see their primary identities as that of remediator and diagnostician. As such, their view of their professional selves is predicated on the assumption that children with disabilities are deficient and need "fixing."[10] Research also indicates that educators of children of color often view themselves as "saviors" whose role it is to "save" youth of color, particularly those living in poverty, by giving the children the help that they need to avoid failing.[11] More specifically, Siuty et al. (2024) conceptualize "white ability saviorism," whereby educators—often white and nondisabled—view themselves as "[heroes] on the basis of their ability to teach students to reproduce white, normative, nondisabled knowledges and ways of being."[12] These savior and remediator positionalities that many educators of children of color with disabilities adopt orient educators toward trying to change children rather than loving them for who they are.

I argue that the transformative, DisCrit-oriented vision for inclusion presented in this book will be liberating not only for children of color with disabilities, but also for their teachers. When educators see their role as that of "heroes" who change the perceived "lesser" humans to be more like them, they are destined to engage in continuous power struggles with their brilliant children of color with disabilities, who will resist such oppressive positionings each day. The educator who relinquishes control and values children of color with disabilities as they are is free to just enjoy students. Like the teachers described in this book, such teachers get to activate their creativity, analytic skills, and authentic caring for others. They then get to delight in the genuine joy experienced by their students of color with disabilities. Freedom dreaming to (re)imagine inclusion to be more liberatory is thus meant to give greater joy and power to both children of color with disabilities *and* their teachers.

In his 2020 book *Begin Again,* Eddie Glaude writes about how imagination was critical for enslaved Black people to "[break] free from the world as it was, because *they imagined the world as it could be.* If the enslaved gave over that power to white masters, especially the power to imagine and to love, black people would not have survived this place."[13] I believe that the children of color with disabilities who resist the racist, ableist status quo of schooling do so because they imagine a different world for themselves. This is how they survive the oppression that they experience every day in school—by believing that a more liberatory and just future is possible. I invite all educators of children of color with disabilities to join with their students in imagining a different world of schooling.

(Re)Imagining inclusion is needed for everyone's survival, children and educators alike. The pervasive medicalized, pathologizing nature of schooling causes harm to all stakeholders. Taking the DisCrit Pedagogy and DisCrit Solidarity practices described in this book and developing their own approach to DisCrit inclusion will give educators "the power to imagine and to love," which is needed to create communities of belonging for children of color with disabilities.

WHAT POLICY MAKERS CAN DO TO (RE)IMAGINE INCLUSION

For inclusion to be (re)imagined for children of color with disabilities in long-lasting, sustainable ways, shifts in educators' practices must be paired with systemic changes. Historically, the problem of disproportionate exclusion of children of color with disabilities has been addressed through what I consider to be "gotcha" policies. These are policies that direct state and local education agencies to identify and hold accountable schools or districts that do not adhere to a particular regulation. For example, in the 1997 reauthorization of the Individuals with Disabilities in Education Act (IDEA), racial inequity in special education was first recognized as a problem and states were mandated to examine disproportionality annually. States were required to measure racial disproportionality in three areas: (1) identification for special education eligibility, (2) placement in particular educational settings, and (3) the incidence, duration, and type of disciplinary action. When racial disproportionality was found in the first two areas of identification and placement, states were required to review and revise policies, practices, and procedures around identification and placement; mandate that the targeted local education agencies allocate appropriate funds to interventions for children belonging to the racial groups found to be disproportionality identified or placed; and require the local education agencies to publicly report on their revised policies, practices, and procedures.[14]

IDEA 2004—the nation's current special education law—includes similar mandates for identifying and holding accountable state and local education agencies where racial disproportionality is present.[15] While the intention of the policy is to encourage reformation of practice and procedures, the policies fail to consider what about the educational conditions surrounding children of color with or suspected of having disabilities might lead to disproportionate identification and exclusion in the first place. The emphasis is on either remediating the policies, practices, and procedures for determining special education eligibility and placement or remediating the children who are disproportionately identified and placed. In other words, the IDEA regulations that have been in effect for the last several decades adopt a medical model approach to addressing the problem of racial disproportionality. The underlying assumption is that if racial disproportionality exists, it must be because the way that children are identified or placed in special education is flawed or the children themselves are failing their way into special education services. So fix the process or fix the children, and the problem will go away.

I believe that a large reason why the problem of disproportionate exclusion of children of color with disabilities has persisted for decades is that pertinent policies do not get at the heart of the issue. What I learned from observing the DisCrit-aligned educators in this book is that true inclusion and belonging happen only when educators actively reject the status quo and they are working in environments that support their doing so. After reading this book, I urge policy makers to ask themselves: *What conditions are needed to make it possible for educators to enact these DisCrit Pedagogy and DisCrit Solidarity practices?* and *What policies can support the creation of such conditions?* Revolutionizing the inclusion classroom such that all children of color with disabilities experience belonging means looking beyond intervening on procedures or children, and instead looking at our collective hearts and minds. Exclusion and isolation persist because children of color with disabilities are not fully seen or valued as they are. *What is it in our humanity that allows us to see another being in this way, and what needs to change about our environment to allow us to see differently?*

Human rights activist and philosopher Grace Lee Boggs (2012) writes in her book *The Next American Revolution:*

> The next American Revolution, at this stage in our history, is not principally about jobs or health insurance or making it possible for more people to realize the American Dream of upward mobility. . . . It is about creating a new American Dream whose goal is a higher Humanity instead of the higher standard of living dependent on Empire. It is about practicing a new, more active, global, and participatory concept of citizenship. It is about becoming the change we wish to see in the world . . . we must have the courage to challenge ourselves to engage in activities that build a new and better world by improving the physical, psychological, political, and spiritual health of ourselves, our families, our communities, our cities, our world, and our planet.[16]

While Boggs was writing primarily about broad economic, health care, and sociopolitical issues, I see many connections between what she calls for and what we need in educational policy to support inclusion and belonging for children of color with disabilities. The American ideals of upward mobility and higher standards of living reflect an individualistic, capitalistic mindset that exists in schools as well. Whiteness and smartness are treated as property, as the corresponding, socially constructed traits earn their owner rights and privileges within school.[17] Children are then forced into a competition where they must show they own traits of whiteness and smartness to be seen as valuable members of the school community. The goal of schooling becomes earning the most property rights, rather than supporting children to be their full selves.

In this kind of environment, educators are also scrambling to be seen as the one who is most effective at helping their students reach the goals of whiteness and smartness. When children do not reach those goals, it affects educators' performance and their sense of identity. They may internalize feelings of failure, which may lead to their blaming the children. The pressure that educators experience in our educational climate, built on high-stakes testing, accountability, and competition, makes them prone to push out children whom they see as impeding their ability to succeed. Schooling today thus breeds unhealthy minds, hearts, and relationships.

What policies might we get if policy makers looked at the problem of disproportionate exclusion of children of color with disabilities with the goal of "a higher Humanity" and a commitment to "improving the physical, psychological, political, and spiritual health of ourselves, our families, our communities, our cities, our world, and our planet"?[18] I argue that policy makers might start with the foundational belief that every child of color with disabilities has the right to learn alongside their nondisabled peers—and to feel loved, valued, and known while doing so. They might then consider what educators need to make this happen, such as . . .

- *School leaders who are committed to inclusion and who have an assets-based approach to thinking about and working with children of color with disabilities*

  Leaders whose feet are held to the fire in a testing- and accountability-driven educational climate cannot adopt this assets-based approach. They will continue to lead out of fear of achievement gaps, which fosters deficit thinking. Policy makers can redirect the emphasis away from high-stakes testing by adjusting the metrics used to determine quality of educational programming. What if joy and belonging were built into measures of educational quality? Or what if love and assets-based thinking were built into teacher evaluation frameworks? Leaders would be more motivated to support their teachers in creating the kind of inclusive environments described in this book.

- *Enough staffing to ensure that every inclusion classroom is equipped with two full-time head teachers and at least one full-time assistant teacher (with more as needed)*
  I often think about the case of Loretta, and how there was no possible way that her teachers could have run after her and given her the time and space that she needed to come back to the classroom of her own accord if there had been only one adult in the room. It is hard to *respect not restrict, make room for the unexpected, center inquiry, recognize the gifts or resistance,* or *center relationship* with your children of color with disabilities when you're alone leading a classroom of twenty to thirty children. Co-teaching classrooms are much more likely to make inclusion not only possible, but enjoyable for everyone involved. Policy makers have the power to ensure that schools and districts receive enough funding to staff their inclusion classrooms adequately so children of color with disabilities can experience belonging.
- *Professional development for teachers on Emotionally Responsive Practice (ERP), Universal Design for Learning (UDL), DisCrit Classroom Ecology principles, letting go of control, and self-care*
  Educational policy often directs the agendas for the professional development that districts and states will offer to their staff. The topics listed here are all concepts that align with the vision for DisCrit Pedagogy and DisCrit Solidarity described in this book.
- *Coaches and counselors for teachers whose primary focus is supporting teacher mental health and well-being*
  As evident in the examples in this book, the work of resisting a system that is oppressive to children of color with disabilities can be emotionally and mentally taxing. When a child behaves in unexpected ways, this can also trigger many different emotions and experiences for educators. For educators to be able to love their children of color with disabilities fully, they also need to feel whole and well. Policy makers can require that state and local education agencies

provide proper professional and mental health support for their teachers. When teachers are stretched too thin, they are less likely to show the care needed to ensure belonging for children of color with disabilities.

- *Curricular and scheduling flexibility to allow teachers to center inquiry more with their children*
  Often, inquiry is not centered in classrooms because of the rigid curriculum standards that teachers are expected to meet and the lack of time that they are given to engage students in long-term (or even short-term) projects. Policy makers can change curriculum standards to build in greater time and flexibility for educators to generate emergent, authentic inquiry with their students.
- *Recognition that our system of schooling is inherently racist and ableist, and efforts made by children or educators to upend this system should not be punished*
  Above all else, policy makers must acknowledge that the system of schooling in the US was designed to oppress children of color with disabilities. It is therefore not enough to simply tell schools and districts not to disproportionately apply disciplinary practices or exclusion to their students of color. Policy makers should welcome the voices of educators and students who are actively resisting the status quo of schooling as they generate new policies. They might engage in authentic dialogue with teachers, families, and children of color with disabilities themselves to collectively cast a vision for educational reform that leads to true inclusion and belonging.

Policies that build on these considerations would promote inclusion and belonging for children of color with disabilities in ways that previous policies have failed to do. Just as you cannot tell a child who is screaming in agony to stop screaming, we cannot continue to simply tell a broken system to stop being broken. It is not enough to wag a finger at schools and say, "Stop disproportionately excluding your children of color with disabilities." Policy makers must think from an ecological, transformational perspective, considering what environmental conditions are needed to allow radical shifts to occur and whose voices must be at the table when policies related to inclusion are generated.

WHAT EDUCATIONAL RESEARCHERS CAN DO TO (RE)IMAGINE INCLUSION

Educational research also has a role to play in pushing forward a movement to (re)imagine inclusion for children of color with disabilities. Much of the literature on children of color with disabilities has focused on their disproportionate representation in special education, as well as their disproportionate exclusion from their nondisabled and white peers. While this line of research has great importance, as it brings attention to serious problems that need to be addressed if social justice is to be achieved, disproportionality research does little to support educators in their day-to-day work with children of color with disabilities and their families.

Like the DisCrit-aligned educators in this book, educational researchers can demonstrate DisCrit Solidarity with children of color with disabilities by seeing their scholarly endeavors as activism. Researchers might engage in community-based participatory action research with educators who are interested in learning more about inclusion and belonging for children of color with disabilities. Rather than solely *studying* problems and questions of interest, researchers can see their work as having the potential to inspire *change*. Research on the disproportionate exclusion of children of color with disabilities can be paired with projects that support educators to enact shifts in their practices that would lead to the gradual development of DisCrit Classroom Ecologies where children of color with disabilities experience belonging.

As educational researchers engage in scholar-activism, they should also center the voices of children of color with disabilities themselves, as well as their families. While the goal of my research was to analyze educator practices, a limitation was the absence of the perspectives and ideas of children and families. Any efforts to (re)imagine inclusion for children of color with disabilities—whether at the pedagogical, policy, or research level—should include the very children who are most affected by such (re)imagining. Children of color with disabilities are the ones who know best what must change in our culture of schooling to ensure that they belong and are no longer pushed out of classrooms and schools.

SOME FINAL WORDS

My daughter was born just as I began writing this book. By the time I finished writing ten months later, she had qualified for early intervention; was diagnosed with ptosis, torticollis, esotropia, and nonspecific chronic ischemic stroke; received months of therapy; and was described by educators and evaluators as "deficient," "delayed," "poor," "below average," and "behind." Although I had worked as a special education teacher, been a researcher and teacher educator in the field of special education, and grown up with family members with disabilities, this pathologizing and deficit-based orientation toward my child was a shock to my system. It is really true that it's different when it's your kid. I felt a newfound urgency about sharing the stories of the DisCrit-aligned educators described in this book. My child is not deficient; she is amazing. My desire for educators to see her brilliance and amazing gifts, as well as my hope that she—as a neurodivergent Asian American child—always knows that she belongs makes (re)imagining inclusion not just a dream I have. It's a necessity.

The problem of disproportionate isolation, exclusion, and segregation of children of color with disabilities has lasted for far too long, with little change. This book shows that this problem is not a hopeless inevitability that cannot go away. The teachers featured in this book and the practices that they demonstrate give me hope that genuine inclusion for children of color with disabilities—children like my daughter—is within reach. Yes, such a radical shift requires commitment, openness, and vulnerability on the parts of educators and policy makers alike. The stories told in this book show us that such commitment, openness, and vulnerability are worth it because they allow children of color with disabilities to experience belonging in their inclusion classrooms, and also allow educators to find joy in their work.

This book puts forth a vision of a more liberatory approach to inclusive practices for children of color with disabilities. Through this (re) imagining, I call on educators and policy makers to embrace pedagogical approaches that recognize and build upon the strengths, interests, and ways of being that children of color with disabilities already have, rather than trying to change them to be more like white nondisabled children. If children of color with disabilities are not forced into conformity but rather are honored in school, then teachers and leaders will not feel the need to push them out of inclusive classrooms. And when children of color with disabilities are free to be themselves, they will thrive.

NOTES

INTRODUCTION

1. Mitchell Yell, "*Brown v. Board of Education* and the Development of Special Education," *Intervention in School and Clinic* 57, no. 3 (2022): 198–200, doi:10.1177/10534512211014874; Mitchell L. Yell, David Rogers, and Elisabeth L. Rogers, "The Legal History of Special Education: What a Long, Strange Trip It's Been!" *Remedial and Special Education* 19, no. 4 (1998): 219–228, doi:10.1177/074193259801900405.
2. Alfredo J. Artiles et al., "Justifying and Explaining Disproportionality, 1968–2008: A Critique of Underlying Views of Culture," *Exceptional Children* 76, no. 3 (2010): 279–299, doi:10.1177/001440291007600303; Subini A. Annamma, David Connor, and Beth Ferri, "Dis/ability Critical Race Studies (DisCrit): Theorizing at the Intersections of Race and Dis/ability," *Race Ethnicity and Education* 16, no. 1 (2013): 1–31, doi:10.1080/13613324.2012.730511; Wanda J. Blanchett, "Disproportionate Representation of African American Students in Special Education: Acknowledging the Role of White Privilege and Racism," *Educational Researcher* 35, no. 6 (2006): 24–28, doi:10.3102/0013189X03500602; Russell J. Skiba et al., "Achieving Equity in Special Education: History, Status, and Current Challenges," *Exceptional Children* 74, no. 3 (2008): 264–288, doi:10.1177/001440290807400301; US Department of Health and Human Services and US Department of Education, "Policy Statement on Inclusion of Children with Disabilities in Early Childhood Programs," September 14, 2015, https://www2.ed.gov/policy/speced/guid/earlylearning/joint-statement-full-text.pdf.
3. US Department of Education, "Special Education—Technical Assistance on State Data Collection," 2022, https://www2.ed.gov/programs/osepidea/618-data/static-tables/index.html#partb-cc.

4. Ambra L. Green, Daniel R. Cohen, and Melissa Stormont, "Addressing and Preventing Disproportionality in Exclusionary Disciplinary Practices for Students of Color with Disabilities," *Intervention in School and Clinic* 54, no. 1 (2018): 241–245, doi:10.1177/1053451218782437; Kevin P. Brady and Suzanne Kucharczyk, "Racial Disproportionality and the Special Education Paradox: The Divide between Legal Compliance and the Best Practice(s)," *384 Education Law Reporter* 585 (2021), https://racism.org/articles/basic-needs/education/44-education-k-12/9366-racial-disproportionality.
5. US Department of Education, "Special Education—Technical Assistance on State Data Collection"; Songtian Zeng et al., "Preschool Suspension and Expulsion for Young Children with Disabilities," *Exceptional Children* 87, no. 2 (2020): 199–216, doi:10.1177/0014402920949832.
6. Artiles et al., "Justifying and Explaining Disproportionality"; Beatriz L. Barrio et al., "Voices beyond the Numbers: A Systematic Review of Qualitative Studies of Disproportionality in Special Education," *Preventing School Failure: Alternative Education for Children and Youth* 67, no. 1 (2023): 39–47, doi:10.1080/1045988X.2022.2101422; North Cooc, "Disparities in the Enrollment and Timing of Special Education for Asian American and Pacific Islander Students," *Journal of Special Education* 53, no. 3 (2019): 1–14, doi:10.1177/0022466919839029; Jennifer Counts, Antonis Katsiyannis, and Denise K. Whitford, "Culturally and Linguistically Diverse Learners in Special Education: English Learners," *NASSP Bulletin* 102, no. 1 (2018), 5–21, doi:10.1177/0192636518755945; Claire E. Kunesh and Amity Noltemeyer, "Understanding Disciplinary Disproportionality: Stereotypes Shape Pre-service Teachers' Beliefs about Black Boys' Behavior," *Urban Education* 54, no. 4 (2019): 471–498, doi:10.1177/0042085915623337; Russell J. Skiba et al., "Risks and Consequences of Oversimplifying Educational Inequities: A Response to Morgan et al. (2015)," *Educational Researcher* 45 (2016): 221–225, doi:10.3102/0013189X16644606; Leanna Stiefel et al., "Who Feels Included in School?" *Educational Researcher* 47, no. 2 (2018): 105–120, doi:10.3102/0013189X17738761; Adai A. Tefera et al., "The Aftermath of Disproportionality Citations: Situating Disability-Race Intersections in Historical, Spatial, and Sociocultural Contexts," *American Educational Research Journal* 60, no. 2 (2023): 367–404, doi:10.3102/00028312221147007.
7. Annamma et al., "Dis/ability Critical Race Studies (DisCrit)."
8. Artiles et al., "Justifying and Explaining Disproportionality."
9. Lloyd M. Dunn, "Special Education for the Mildly Retarded: Is Much of It Justifiable?" *Exceptional Children* 23, no. 35 (1968): 6, doi:10.1177/001440296803500101.
10. Alfredo J. Artiles et al., "Over-identification of Students of Color in Special Education: A Critical Overview," *Multicultural Perspectives* 4, no. 1 (2002): 3–10, doi:10.1207/S15327892MCP0401_2; Artiles et al., "Justifying and

Explaining Disproportionality"; Rebecca A. Cruz, Saili S. Kulkarni, and Allison R. Firestone, "A QuantCrit Analysis of Context, Discipline, Special Education, and Disproportionality," *AERA Open* 7, no. 1 (2021): 1–16, doi:10.1177/23328584211041354; Green et al., "Addressing and Preventing Disproportionality"; Russell J. Skiba et al., "Achieving Equity in Special Education: History, Status, and Current Challenges," *Exceptional Children* 74, no. 3 (2008): 264–288, doi:10.1177/001440290807400301.

11. Annamma et al., "Dis/ability Critical Race Studies (DisCrit)"; Artiles et al., "Justifying and Explaining Disproportionality."
12. Ibid.; Barrio et al., "Voices beyond the Numbers"; Counts et al., "Culturally and Linguistically Diverse Learners"; Cruz et al., "A QuantCrit Analysis"; Beth Harry and Janette Klingner, *Why Are So Many Minority Students in Special Education? Understanding Race and Disability in Schools* (New York: Teachers College Press, 2014); Janette K. Klingner et al., "Addressing the Disproportionate Representation of Culturally and Linguistically Diverse Students in Special Education through Culturally Responsive Educational Systems," *Education Policy Analysis Archives* 13, no. 38 (2005): 1–40, doi:10.14507/epaa.v13n38.2005; Amanda L. Sullivan and Aydin Bal, "Disproportionality in Special Education: Effects of Individual and School Variables on Disability Risk," *Exceptional Children* 79, no. 4 (2013): 475–494, doi:10.1177/001440291307900406; Adai A. Tefera and Gustavo E. Fischman, "How and Why Context Matters in the Study of Racial Disproportionality in Special Education: Toward a Critical Disability Education Policy Approach," *Equity & Excellence in Education* 53, no. 4 (2020): 434–449, doi:10.1080/10665684.2020.1791284.
13. Alfredo J. Artiles, "Toward an Interdisciplinary Understanding of Educational Equity and Difference: The Case of the Racialization of Ability," *Educational Researcher* 40, no. 9 (2011): 431–445, doi: 10.3102/0013189X11429391; North Cooc, "Examining the Underrepresentation of Asian Americans in Special Education: New Trends from California School Districts," *Exceptionality* 26, no.1 (2016): 1–19, doi:10.1080/09362835.2016.1216847; Cooc, "Disparities in the Enrollment and Timing of Special Education"; Deborah A. Hwa-Froelich and Carol E. Westby, "Frameworks of Education: Perspectives of Southeast Asian Parents and Head Start Staff," *Language, Speech, and Hearing Services in Schools 34,* no. 4 (2003): 299–319, doi:10.1044/0161-1461(2003/025); Soyoung Park, "Beyond Underrepresentation: Constructing Disability with Young Asian American Children to Preserve the 'Model Minority' Stereotype," *Asia-Pacific Journal of Research in Early Childhood Education* 13, no. 3 (2019): 73–95, doi:10.17206/apjrece.2019.13.3.73.
14. Barrio et al., "Voices beyond the Numbers"; Counts et al., "Culturally and Linguistically Diverse Learners"; Harry and Klingner, *Why Are So Many Minority Students in Special Education?*; Soyoung Park, "Demystifying Disproportionality: Exploring Educator Beliefs about Special Education

Referrals for English Learners," *Teachers College Record* 122, no. 5 (2020): 1–40, doi:10.1177/016146812012200510; Skiba et al., "Achieving Equity in Special Education"; Leanna Stiefel et al., "The Role of School Context in Explaining Racial Disproportionality in Special Education," NYU Wagner research paper (October 2022): 1–61, doi:10.2139/ssrn.4318607; Tefera and Fischman, "How and Why Context Matters."

15. Jennifer K. Adair and Kiyomi S. Colegrove, *Segregation by Experience: Agency, Racism, and Learning in the Early Grades* (Chicago: University of Chicago Press, 2021), 2.
16. Adair and Colegrove, *Segregation by Experience,* 3. Daphan Bassok, Scott Latham, & Anna Rorem, "Is Kindergarten the New First Grade?" *AERA Open 2*, no. 1 (2016). https://doi.org/10.1177/2332858415616358.
17. Christine Sleeter, "Multicultural Education vs. Factory Model Schooling," in *Multicultural Education: A Renewed Paradigm of Transformation and Call to Action,* ed. H. Prentice Baptiste (San Francisco: Caddo Gap Press, 2015), 3.
18. Ray McDermott, Shelley Goldman, and Hervé Varenne, "The Cultural Work of Learning Disbilities," *Educational Researcher* 35, no. 6, 12.
19. McDermott et al., "The Cultural Work of Learning Disbilities."
20. Adair and Colegrove, *Segregation by Experience.*
21. North Cooc, "Disparities in General Education Inclusion for Students of Color with Disabilities: Understanding When and Why," *Journal of School Psychology* 90 (2022): 43–59, doi:10.1016/j.jsp.2021.10.002.
22. Counts et al., "Culturally and Linguistically Diverse Learners"; Skiba et al., "Achieving Equity in Special Education"; Amanda L. Sullivan and Aydin Bal, "Disproportionality in Special Education: Effects of Individual and School Variables on Disability Risk," *Exceptional Children* 79, no. 4 (2013): 475–494, doi:10.1177/001440291307900406.
23. Patrick Howard, "The Least Restrictive Environment: How to Tell?" *Journal of Law & Education* 33, no. 2 (2004): 167–180; Laura O'Laughlin and Jane C. Lindle, "Principals as Political Agents in the Implementation of IDEA's Least Restrictive Environment Mandate," *Educational Policy* 29, no. 1 (2015): 140–161, doi:10.1177/0895904814563207; Yell et al., "The Legal History of Special Education."
24. Stacey Gordon, "Making Sense of the Inclusion Debate under IDEA," *Brigham Young University Education and Law Journal* 189 (2006): 189–225, https://digitalcommons.law.byu.edu/elj/vol2006/iss1/5; Margaret A. Winzer, *From Integration to Inclusion: A History of Special Education in the 20th Century* (Washington, DC: Gallaudet University Press, 2009).
25. David J. Connor and Beth A. Ferri, "The Conflict Within: Resistance to Inclusion and Other Paradoxes in Special Education," *Disability and Society* 22, no. 1 (2007): 63–77, doi:10.1080/09687590601056717; Kenneth A. Kavale and Stephen R. Forness, "History, Rhetoric, and Reality: Analysis of the

Inclusion Debate," *Remedial and Special Education* 21, no. 5 (2000): 279–296, doi:10.1177/074193250002100505; Robert L. Osgood, *The History of Inclusion in the United States* (Washington, DC: Gallaudet University Press, 2009); Winzer, *From Integration to Inclusion.*

26. Yell, "*Brown v. Board of Education.*"
27. Jean B. Crockett and James M. Kauffman, *The Least Restrictive Environment: Its Origins and Interpretations in Special Education* (Mahwah, NJ: Lawrence Erlbaum Associates, 1999).
28. Michael F. Giangreco, "'How Can a Student with Severe Disabilities Be in a Fifth-Grade Class When He Can't Do Fifth-Grade Level Work?' Misapplying the Least Restrictive Environment," *Research and Practice for Persons with Severe Disabilities* 45, no. 1 (2020): 23–27, doi:10.1177/1540796919892733; Steven J. Taylor, "Caught in the Continuum: A Critical Analysis of the Principal of the Least Restrictive Environment," *Journal of the Association for the Severely Handicapped* 13, no. 1 (1988): 41–53, doi:10.2511/rpsd.29.4.218.
29. Marian P. B. Francisco, Maria Hartman, and Ye Wang, "Inclusion and Special Education," *Education Sciences* 10, no. 9 (2020): 238, doi:10.3390/educsci10090238; Teri A. Marx et al., "Guiding IEP Teams on Meeting the Least Restrictive Environment Mandate," *Intervention in School and Clinic* 50, no. 1 (2014): 45–50, doi:10.1177/1053451214532345.
30. Individuals with Disabilities in Education Improvement Act of 2004, Pub. L. No. 108-446, 118 Stat. 2647 (2004).
31. Turki A. Alquraini, "An Analysis of Legal Issues Relating to the Least Restrictive Environment Standards," *Journal of Research in Special Education Needs* 13, no. 2 (2013): 152–158, doi:10.1111/j.1471-3802.2011.01220.x; Howard, "The Least Restrictive Environment"; Taylor, "Caught in the Continuum"; Julie Underwood, "Under the Law: Defining the Least Restrictive Environment," *Phi Delta Kappan* 100, no. 3 (2018): 66–67, doi:10.1177/0031721718808270.
32. Soyoung Park, "Thickening Borders through Least Restrictive Environment: The Case of an Immigrant Kindergartner with Autism," *Multiple Voices: Disability, Race, and Language Intersections in Special Education* 23, no. 1 (2023): 4–19, doi:10.56829/2158-396X-23.1.4; Janet S. Sauer and Cheryl M. Jorgensen, "Still Caught in the Continuum: A Critical Analysis of Least Restrictive Environment and Its Effects on Placement of Students with Intellectual Disability," *Inclusion* 4, no. 2 (2016): 56–74, doi:10.1352/2326-6988-4.2.56.
33. Giangreco, "How Can a Student with Severe Disabilities Be in a Fifth-Grade Class?"; Park, "Thickening Borders through Least Restrictive Environment."
34. Akul Gupta et al., "Individualized Education Program (IEP) under Examination: A Literature Review of Systemic Flaws in Education for Students with Disabilities," *SSRN Electronic Journal*, 2023: 1–16, doi:10.2139/ssrn.4508281; Yell et al., "The Legal History of Special Education."

35. Dawn A. Rowe and Grace L. Francis, "Reflective Thinking: Considering the Intersection of Microcultures in IEP Planning and Implementation," *Teaching Exceptional Children* 53, no. 1 (2020), doi:10.1177/004005992095200.
36. Adrian Woo Jung, "Individualized Education Programs (IEPs) and Barriers for Parents from Culturally and Linguistically Diverse Backgrounds," *Multicultural Education 19*, no. 3 (2011): 21–25, https://eric.ed.gov/?id=EJ955935.
37. US Department of Education, "Special Education—Technical Assistance on State Data Collection."
38. Gordon, "Making Sense of the Inclusion Debate"; Francisco et al., "Inclusion and Special Education"; Underwood, "Under the Law."
39. Alfredo J. Artiles and Elizabeth B. Kozleski, "Beyond Convictions: Interrogating Culture, History, and Power in Inclusive Education," *Language Arts* 84, no. 4 (2007): 357–364. http://hdl.handle.net/1808/10881; Francisco et al., "Inclusion and Special Education"; Megan McGovern, "Least Restrictive Environment: Fulfilling the Promises of IDEA," *Widener Law Review* 21, no. 117 (2015): 117–137, https://widenerlawreview.org/files/2015/02/10-McGovern-1.pdf; Mara Sapon-Shevin, *Widening the Circle: The Power of Inclusive Classrooms* (Boston: Beacon Press, 2007).
40. Giangreco, "How Can a Student with Severe Disabilities Be in a Fifth-Grade Class?"; Robert Rueda, Margaret A. Gallego, and Luis C. Moll, "The Least Restrictive Environment: A Place or a Context?" *Remedial and Special Education* 21, no. 2 (2000): 70–78, doi:10.1177/074193250002100202; Sauer and Jorgensen, "Still Caught in the Continuum."
41. Artiles and Kozleski, "Beyond Convictions," 357.
42. Subini Annamma and Deb Morrison, "DisCrit Classroom Ecology: Using Praxis to Dismantle Dysfunctional Education Ecologies," *Teaching and Teacher Education* 73 (2018): 70–80, doi:10.1016/j.tate.2018.03.008.
43. Annamma and Morrison, "DisCrit Classroom Ecology," 75.
44. Susan Baglieri, *Disability Studies and the Inclusive Classroom: Critical Practices for Embracing Diversity in Education*, 2nd ed. (New York: Routledge, 2017).
45. Susan Baglieri et al., "Disability Studies in Education: The Need for a Plurality of Perspectives on Disability," *Remedial and Special Education* 32, no. 4 (2011): 267–278, doi:10.1177/0741932510362200.
46. Annamma et al., "Dis/ability Critical Race Studies (DisCrit)"; Annamma and Morrison, "DisCrit Classroom Ecology."
47. Christine L. Hancock, Chelsea W. Morgan, and James Holly Jr., "Counteracting Dysconscious Racism and Ableism through Fieldwork: Applying DisCrit Classroom Ecology in Early Childhood Personnel Preparation," *Topics in Early Childhood Special Education* 41, no. 1 (2021): 45–56, doi:10.1177/0271121421 989797.
48. Annamma and Morrison, "DisCrit Classroom Ecology"; Hancock et al., "Counteracting Dysconscious Racism and Ableism."

49. Valentina Migliarini and Chelsea Stinson, "A Disability Critical Race Theory Solidarity Approach to Transform Pedagogy and Classroom Culture in TESOL," *TESOL Quarterly* 55, no. 3 (2021): 708–718, doi:10.1002/tesq.3028.

CHAPTER 1

1. Bradley A. Areheart, "When Disability Isn't 'Just Right': The Entrenchment of the Medical Model of Disability and the *Goldilocks* Dilemma," *Indiana Law Journal* 83, no. 181 (2008): 181–232; Susan Baglieri, *Disability Studies and the Inclusive Classroom: Critical Practices for Embracing Diversity in Education*, 2nd ed. (New York: Routledge, 2017); Zosia Zaks, "Changing the Medical Model of Disability to the Normalization Model of Disability: Clarifying the Past to Create a New Future Direction," *Disability and Society* (2023): 1–28, doi:10.1080/09687599.2023.2255926.
2. Andrew J. Hogan, "Moving Away from the 'Medical Model': The Development and Revision of the World Health Organization's Classification of Disability," *Bulletin of the History of Medicine* 93, no. 2 (2019): 241–269, doi:10.1353/bhm.2019.0028; Zaks, "Changing the Medical Model."
3. Susan Baglieri et al., "Disability Studies in Education: The Need for a Plurality of Perspectives on Disability," *Remedial and Special Education* 32, no. 4 (2011): 267–278, doi:10.1177/0741932510362200.
4. Baglieri et al., "Disability Studies in Education"; Justin A. Haegele and Samuel Hodge, "Disability Discourse: Overview and Critiques of the Medical and Social Models," *Quest* 68, no. 2 (2016): 193–206, doi:10.1080/00336297.2016.1143849; David Pfeiffer, "The Philosophical Foundations of Disability Studies," *Disability Studies Quarterly* 22, no. 2 (2002): 3–23, doi:10.18061/dsq.v22i2.341; Tom Shakespeare, "The Social Model of Disability," in *The Disability Studies Reader (4th Ed.)*, ed. Lennard J. Davis (New York: Routledge, 2013), 214–221.
5. Sophie Mitra, "The Capability Approach and Disability," *Journal of Disability Policy Studies* 16, no. 4 (2006): 236–247, doi:10.1177/10442073060160040501; Pfeiffer, "The Philosophical Foundations of Disability Studies"; Zaks, "Changing the Medical Model of Disability."
6. Ellen Brantlinger, "Confounding the Needs and Confronting the Norms: An Extension of Reid and Valle's Essay," *Journal of Learning Disabilities* 37, no. 6 (2004): 490–499, doi:10.1177/00222194040370060301; Haegele and Hodge, "Disability Discourse"; Zaks, "Changing the Medical Model of Disability."
7. Wanda J. Blanchett, Janette K. Klingner, and Beth Harry, "The Intersection of Race, Culture, Language, and Disability: Implications for Urban Education," *Urban Education, 44*(4) (2009): 389–409, doi:10.1177/0042085909338686; North Cooc, "Disparities in General Education Inclusion for Students of Color with Disabilities: Understanding When and Why," *Journal of School Psychology* 90 (2022): 43–59, doi:10.1016/j.jsp.2021.10.002.

8. Martin Agran et al., "Why Aren't Students with Severe Disabilities Being Placed in General Education Classrooms: Examining the Relations among Classroom Placement, Learner Outcomes, and Other Factors," *Research and Practice for Persons with Severe Disabilities* 45, no. 1 (2020): 4–13, doi:1.o0r.g1/107.171/1775/41054709769961991988778813 4.
9. "Special Education—Technical Assistance on State Data Collection," US Department of Education (2022), https://www2.ed.gov/programs/osepidea/618-data/static-tables/index.html#partb-cc.
10. Alfie Kohn, *Punished by Rewards: The Trouble with Gold Stars, Incentive Plans, A's, Praise, and Other Bribes (Twenty-Fifth Anniversary Ed.)* (Boston: Houghton Mifflin, 2018).
11. Baglieri et al., "Disability Studies in Education."
12. David J. Connor et al., "Disability Studies and Inclusive Education: Implications for Theory, Research, and Practice," *International Journal of Inclusive Education* 12, no. 5–6 (2008): 441–457, doi:10.1080/13603110802377482.
13. Eric Shyman, "The Reinforcement of Ableism: Normality, the Medical Model of Disability, and Humanism in Applied Behavior Analysis and ASD," *Intellectual and Developmental Disabilities* 54, no. 5 (2016): 366–376, doi:10.1352/1934-9556-54.5.366.
14. Susan Baglieri et al., "(Re)claiming 'Inclusive Education' toward Cohesion in Educational Reform: Disability Studies Unravels the Myth of the Normal Child," *Teachers College Record* 113, no. 10 (2011): 2122–2154, doi:10.1177/016146811111301001. Zaks, "Changing the Medical Model."
15. Django Paris, "Culturally Sustaining Pedagogy: A Needed Change in Stance, Terminology, and Practice," *Educational Researcher* 41, no. 3 (2012): 93, doi:10.3102/0013189X12441244.
16. Peter McLaren, "The Future of Critical Pedagogy," *Educational Philosophy and Theory* 52, no. 12 (2020): 1243, doi: 10.1080/00131857.2019.1686963.
17. Peter McLaren, "Critical Pedagogy: A Look at Major Concepts," in *The Critical Pedagogy Reader,* ed. Antonia Darder et al. (New York: RoutlegeFalmer, 2002), 69–96. http://ereserve.library.utah.edu/Annual/WRTG/3015/Lenart/fromped.pdf
18. Peter McLaren, "Schooling the Postmodern Body: Critical Pedagogy and the Politics of Enfleshment," *Journal of Education* 170, no. 3 (1988): 62, https://www.jstor.org/stable/42748648.
19. Michael A. Peters and Tina (A. C.) Besley, "Introduction: Why Foucault? New Directions in Educational Research," in *Why Foucault? New Directions in Educational Research,* ed. Michael A. Peters and Tina (A. C.) Besley (New York: Peter Lang, 2008), 1–14.
20. Michel Foucault, *The Foucault Reader* (New York: Pantheon Books, 1984).
21. Subini A. Annamma et al., "Black Girls and School Discipline: The Complexities of Being Overrepresented and Understudied," *Urban Education* 54, no. 2

(2019): 211–242, doi:10.1177/0042085916646610; Nirmala Erevelles, "Crippin' Jim Crow: Disability, Dis-location, and the School-to-Prison Pipeline," in *Disability Incarcerated,* ed. Liat Ben-Moshe et al. (New York: Palgrave Macmillan, 2014), 81–99, doi:10.1057/9781137388476_5.

22. Maria Cioè-Peña, "Raciolinguistics and the Education of Emergent Bilinguals Labeled as Disabled," *Urban Review* 53 (2021): 443–469, doi:10.1007/s11256-020-00581-z; Soyoung Park, "Thickening Borders through Least Restrictive Environment: The Case of an Immigrant Kindergartner with Autism," *Multiple Voices: Disability, Race, and Language Intersections in Special Education* 23, no. 1 (2023): 4–19, doi:10.56829/2158-396X-23.1.4.
23. Soyoung Park, "Beyond Underrepresentation: Constructing Disability with Young Asian American Children to Preserve the 'Model Minority' Stereotype," *Asia-Pacific Journal of Research in Early Childhood Education* 13, no. 3 (2019): 73–95, doi:10.17206/apjrece.2019.13.3.73.
24. Gloria S. Boutte and George L. Johnson Jr., "*Funga alafia*: Toward Welcoming, Understanding, and Respecting African American Speakers' Bilingualism and Biliteracy," *Equity and Excellence in Education* 46, no. 3 (2013): 300–314, doi:10.1080/10665684.2013.806850.
25. Patricia Martínez-Àlvarez, "Dis/ability as Mediator: Opportunity Encounters in Hybrid Learning Spaces for Emergent Bilinguals with Dis/abilities," *Teachers College Record* 122, no. 5 (2020): 1–44, doi:10.1177/016146812012200506.
26. Cioè-Peña, "Raciolinguistics and the Education of Emergent Bilinguals."
27. Cioè-Peña, *(M)othering Labeled Children* (Blue Ridge Summit: Multilingual Matters, 2021).
28. Martínez-Àlvarez, "Dis/ability as Mediator."

CHAPTER 2

1. Subini A. Annamma, David Connor, and Beth Ferri, "Dis/ability Critical Race Studies (DisCrit): Theorizing at the Intersections of Race and Dis/ability," *Race Ethnicity and Education* 16, no. 1 (2013): 6, doi:10.1080/13613324.2012.730511.
2. Subini Annamma and Deb Morrison, "DisCrit Classroom Ecology: Using Praxis to Dismantle Dysfunctional Education Ecologies," *Teaching and Teacher Education* 73, (2018): 70–80, doi:10.1016/j.tate.2018.03.008; Subini Annamma and Deb Morrison, "Identifying Dysfunctional Education Ecologies: A DisCrit Analysis of Bias in the Classroom," *Equity & Excellence in Education* 51, no. 2 (2018): 114–131, doi:10.1080/10665684.2018.1496047.
3. Ibid; Annamma and Morrison, "DisCrit Classroom Ecology"; Annamma and Morrison, "Identfying Dysfunctional Education Ecologies"; Christine L. Hancock, Chelsea W. Morgan, and James Holly Jr., "Counteracting Dysconscious Racism and Ableism through Fieldwork: Applying DisCrit Classroom Ecology in Early Childhood Personnel Preparation," *Topics in Early Childhood Special Education* 41, no. 1 (2021): 45–56, doi:10.1177/0271121421989797.

4. Annamma et al., "Dis/ability Critical Race Studies (DisCrit)," 11.
5. Annamma and Morrison, "DisCrit Classroom Ecology," 75–76.
6. Hancock et al., "Counteracting Dysconscious Racism and Ableism," 51; Center for Applied Special Technology (CAST), "Universal Design for Learning Guidelines Version 2.0." (2011). http://udlguidelines.cast.org/more/downloads; Frederico R. Waitoller and Kathleen K. Thorius, "Cross-Pollinating Culturally Sustaining Pedagogy and Universal Design for Learning: Toward an Inclusive Pedagogy that Accounts for Dis/Ability," *Harvard Educational Review* 86, no. 3 (2016): 366-389, doi:10.17763/1943-5045-86.3.366.
7. CAST, "About Universal Design for Learning," last modified 2024, https://www.cast.org/impact/universal-design-for-learning-udl.
8. Valentina Migliarini and Subini Annamma, "Applying Disability Critical Race Theory in the Practice of Teacher Education in the United States," in *Oxford Encyclopedia of Global Perspectives on Teacher Education,* ed. Jo Lampert (Oxford: Oxford University Press, 2019): 8, doi:10.1093/acrefore/9780190264093.013.783.
9. Annamma and Morrison, "DisCrit Classroom Ecology," 76–77.
10. Subini A. Annamma and Tamara Handy, "DisCrit Solidarity as Curriculum Studies and Transformative Praxis," *Curriculum Inquiry* 49, no. 4 (2019): 442–463, doi:10.1080/03626784.2019.1665456.
11. Annamma and Handy, "DisCrit Solidarity as Curriculum Studies and Transformative Praxis": 454.
12. Annamma and Morrison, "DisCrit Classroom Ecology"; Annamma and Morrison, "Identifying Dysfunctional Education Ecologies"; Hancock et al., "Counteracting Dysconscious Racism and Ableism"; Meaghan Krazinski and Brenda Flores, "Classrooms as Healing Spaces," *Journal of Trauma Studies in Education* 2, no. 1 (2023): 145–163, doi:10.32674/jtse.v2i1.3898; Valentina Migliarini and Subini A. Annamma, "Classroom and Behavior Management: (Re)conceptualizing through Disability Critical Race Theory," in *Handbook on Promoting Social Justice in Education,* ed. Rosemary Papa (Cham, Switzerland: Springer, Cham, 2019), 1–22, doi:10.1007/978-3-319-74078-2_95-1.
13. Migliarini and Annamma, "Applying Disability Critical Race Theory," 12.
14. Annamma and Handy, "DisCrit Solidarity as Curriculum Studies."
15. Frederick Erickson, "Qualitative Methods in Research on Teaching," in *The Handbook of Research on Teaching,* ed. Merlin C. Wittrock (New York: Macmillan, 1986), 119–161; Sharan B. Merriam, *Qualitative Research: A Guide to Design and Implementation* (Hoboken, NJ: Jossey-Bass, 2009).
16. Robert M. Emerson, Rachel I. Fretz, and Linda L. Shaw, *Writing Ethnographic Fieldnotes,* 2nd ed. (Chicago: University of Chicago Press, 2011).
17. Michael Williams and Tami Moser, "The Art of Coding and Thematic Exploration in Qualitative Research," *International Management Review* 15, no. 1

(2019): 45–55, http://www.imrjournal.org/uploads/1/4/2/8/14286482/imr-v15n1art4.pdf.

18. John W. Creswell, *Quantitative, Qualitative, and Mixed Methods Approaches,* 4th ed. (Thousand Oaks, CA: SAGE Publications, 2014).

CHAPTER 3

1. Subini Annamma and Deb Morrison, "DisCrit Classroom Ecology: Using Praxis to Dismantle Dysfunctional Education Ecologies," *Teaching and Teacher Education* 73, (2018): 75, doi:10.1016/j.tate.2018.03.008.
2. CAST, "About Universal Design for Learning," last modified 2024, Christine L. Hancock, Chelsea W. Morgan, and James Holly Jr., "Counteracting Dysconscious Racism and Ableism through Fieldwork: Applying DisCrit Classroom Ecology in Early Childhood Personnel Preparation," *Topics in Early Childhood Special Education* 41, no. 1 (2021): 45–56, doi:10.1177/0271121421989797.
3. Subini Annamma and Deb Morrison, "DisCrit Classroom Ecology: Using Praxis to Dismantle Dysfunctional Education Ecologies," *Teaching and Teacher Education* 73, (2018): 75, doi:10.1016/j.tate.2018.03.008.
4. Gloria Ladson-Billings, *The Dreamkeepers: Successful Teachers of African American Children,* 2nd ed. (Hoboken, NJ: Jossey-Bass, 2009).
5. bell hooks, *All about Love: New Visions* (New York: William Morrow, 2001), 4–5.

CHAPTER 4

1. Subini Annamma and Deb Morrison, "DisCrit Classroom Ecology: Using Praxis to Dismantle Dysfunctional Education Ecologies," *Teaching and Teacher Education* 73 (2018): 76, doi:10.1016/j.tate.2018.03.008.

CHAPTER 5

1. Jane T. Broderick and Seong Bock Hong, *From Children's Interests to Children's Thinking: Using a Cycle of Inquiry to Plan Curriculum* (Washington, DC: National Association for the Education of Young Children, 2020), 1.

CHAPTER 6

1. Subini A. Annamma and Deb Morrison, "DisCrit Classroom Ecology: Using Praxis to Dismantle Dysfunctional Education Ecologies," *Teaching and Teacher Education* 73 (2018): 77, doi:10.1016/j.tate.2018.03.008.
2. Subini A. Annamma and Tamara Handy, "DisCrit Solidarity as Curriculum Studies and Transformative Praxis," *Curriculum Inquiry* 49, no. 4 (2019): 442–463, doi:10.1080/03626784.2019.1665456.
3. Carla Shalaby, *Troublemakers* (New York: The New Press, 2017), xxi.
4. Valentina Migliarini and Subini A. Annamma, "Classroom and Behavior Management: (Re)conceptualizing through Disability Critical Race

Theory," in *Handbook on Promoting Social Justice in Education*, ed. Rosemary Papa (Cham, Switzerland: Springer Cham, 2019), 1–22, doi:10.1007/978-3-319-74078-2_95-1.

5. Annamma and Morrison, "DisCrit Classroom Ecology," 77.
6. Subini A. Annamma, David Connor, and Beth Ferri, "Dis/ability Critical Race Studies (DisCrit): Theorizing at the Intersections of Race and Dis/ability," *Race Ethnicity and Education* 16, no. 1 (2013): 11, doi:10.1080/13613324.2012.730511.
7. Subini A. Annamma et al., "Black Girls and School Discipline: The Complexities of Being Overrepresented and Understudied," *Urban Education* 54, no. 2 (2019): 211–242, doi:10.1177/0042085916646610; Nirmala Erevelles, "Crippin' Jim Crow: Disability, Dis-location, and the School-to-Prison Pipeline," in *Disability Incarcerated*, ed. Liat Ben-Moshe et al. (New York: Palgrave Macmillan, 2014), 81–99, doi:10.1057/9781137388476_5.
8. Lesley Koplow, *Emotionally Responsive Practice: A Path for Schools That Heal, Infancy-Grade 6* (New York: Teachers College Press, 2021), 4.
9. Meaghan Krazinski and Brenda Flores, "Classrooms as Healing Spaces," *Journal of Trauma Studies in Education* 2, no. 1 (2023): 145–163, doi:10.32674/jtse.v2i1.3898.
10. Koplow, *Emotionally Responsive Practice*, 61.
11. Annamma and Handy, "DisCrit Solidarity as Curriculum Studies," 455.
12. Subini A. Annamma, Beth A. Ferri, and David J. Connor, *DisCrit Expanded: Reverberations, Ruptures, and Inquiries* (New York: Teachers College Press, 2022), 4.
13. Annamma and Morrison, "DisCrit Classroom Ecology."
14. Krazinski and Flores, "Classrooms as Healing Spaces."
15. Krazinski and Flores, "Classrooms as Healing Spaces."

CHAPTER 7

1. Subini A. Annamma and Tamara Handy, "DisCrit Solidarity as Curriculum Studies and Transformative Praxis," *Curriculum Inquiry* 49, no. 4 (2019): 449, doi:10.1080/03626784.2019.1665456.
2. bell hooks, *All about Love: New Visions* (New York: William Morrow, 2001), 5.
3. hooks, *All about Love*, 159.
4. Valentina Migliarini and Subini Annamma, "Applying Disability Critical Race Theory in the Practice of Teacher Education in the United States," in *Oxford Encyclopedia of Global Perspectives on Teacher Education*, ed. Jo Lampert (Oxford: Oxford University Press, 2019), 11, doi:10.1093/acrefore/9780190264093.013.783.
5. hooks, *All about Love*, xxiv.
6. hooks, *All about Love*, 5.
7. hooks, *All about Love*, 221.

CONCLUSION

1. Subini A. Annamma, Beth A. Ferri, and David J. Connor, *DisCrit Expanded: Reverberations, Ruptures, and Inquiries* (New York: Teachers College Press, 2022), 2.
2. Susan Baglieri et al., "Disability Studies in Education: The Need for a Plurality of Perspectives on Disability," *Remedial and Special Education* 32, no. 4 (2011): 267–278, doi:10.1177/0741932510362200; Justin A. Haegele and Samuel Hodge, "Disability Discourse: Overview and Critiques of the Medical and Social Models," *Quest* 68, no. 2 (2016): 193–206, doi:10.1080/00336297.2016.1143849; David Pfeiffer, "The Philosophical Foundations of Disability Studies," *Disability Studies Quarterly* 22, no. 2 (2002): 3–23, doi:10.18061/dsq.v22i2.341; Tom Shakespeare, "The Social Model of Disability," in *The Disability Studies Reader (4th Ed.),* ed. Lennard J. Davis (New York: Routledge, 2013), 214–221.
3. Bettina L. Love, *We Want to Do More than Survive: Abolitionist Teaching and the Pursuit of Educational Freedom* (Boston: Beacon Press, 2019), 101.
4. Love, *We Want to Do More than Survive,* 103.
5. Love, *We Want to Do More than Survive,* 101.
6. Diana D. Schaack, Vi-Nhuan Le, and Jennifer Stedron, "When Fulfillment Is Not Enough: Early Childhood Teacher Occupational Burnout and Turnover Intentions from a Job Demands and Resources Perspective," *Early Education and Development* 31, no. 7 (2020): 1011–1030, doi:10.1080/10409289.2020.1791648; Sheila Smith and Sharmila M. Lawrence, "Early Care and Education Teacher Well-being: Associations with Children's Experience, Outcomes, and Workplace Conditions: A Research-to-Policy Brief," *Child Care & Early Education Research Connections* (2019): 1–17, doi:10.7916/d8-ngw9-n011; Melissa Stormont and Laine Young-Walker, "Supporting Professional Development Needs for Early Childhood Teachers: An Exploratory Analysis of Teacher Perceptions of Stress and Challenging Behavior," *International Journal on Disability and Human Development* 16, no.1 (2016): 99–104, doi:10.1515/ijdhd-2016-0037.
7. Subini A. Annamma, David Connor, and Beth Ferri, "Dis/ability Critical Race Studies (DisCrit): Theorizing at the Intersections of Race and Dis/ability," *Race Ethnicity and Education* 16, no. 1 (2013): 12, doi:10.1080/13613324.2012.730511.
8. Valentina Migliarini and Subini Annamma, "Applying Disability Critical Race Theory in the Practice of Teacher Education in the United States," in *Oxford Encyclopedia of Global Perspectives on Teacher Education,* ed. Jo Lampert (Oxford: Oxford University Press, 2019), 5, doi:10.1093/acrefore/9780190264093.013.783.
9. Migliarini and Annamma, "Applying Disability Critical Race Theory," 8.
10. Kathleen A. K. Thorius, "Stimulating Tensions in Special Education Teachers' Figured World: An Approach toward Inclusive Education," *International*

Journal of Inclusive Education 20, no. 12 (2016): 1326–1343, doi:10.1080/13603116.2016.1168877.

11. Brittany A. Aronson, "The White Savior Industrial Complex: A Cultural Studies Analysis of a Teacher Educator, Savior Film, and Future Teachers," *Journal of Critical Thought and Praxis* 6, no. 3 (2017): 36–54, doi:10.31274/jctp-180810-83; Amy Brown, "Waiting for Superwoman: White Female Teachers and the Construction of the 'Neoliberal Savior' in a New York City Public School," *Journal for Critical Education Policy Studies* 11, no. 2 (2013): 123–164, http://www.jceps.com/wp-content/uploads/PDFs/11-2-05.pdf; Antonio J. Castro, "Visionaries, Reformers, Saviors, and Opportunists: Visions and Metaphors for Teaching in the Urban Schools," *Education and Urban Society 46,* no.1 (2014): 135–160, doi:10.1177/0013124512448671.
12. Molly B. Siuty, Maggie R. Beneke, and Tamara Handy, "Conceptualizing White-Ability Saviorism: A Necessary Reckoning with Ableism in Urban Teacher Education," *Review of Educational Research* 0, no. 0 (2024): 20, https://doi.org/10.3102/00346543241241336.
13. Eddie S. Glaude Jr., *Begin Again: James Baldwin's America and Its Urgent Lessons for Our Own* (New York: Crown, 2020), 210.
14. Individuals with Disabilities Education Act of 1997. Pub. L. No. 105-17, 111 Stat. 37 (1997).
15. Individuals with Disabilities Education Improvement Act of 2004, Pub. L. No. 108-446, 118 Stat. 2647 (2004).
16. Grace Lee Boggs, *The Next American Revolution: Sustainable Activism for the Twenty-First Century* (Berkeley: University of California Press, 2012), 72.
17. Subini A. Annamma, "Whiteness as Property: Innocence and Ability in Teacher Education," *Urban Review* 47, (2015): 293–316, doi:10.1007/s11256-014-0293-6; Zeus Leonardo and Alicia A. Broderick, "Smartness as Property: A Critical Exploration of Intersections between Whiteness and Disability Studies," *Teachers College Record* 113, no. 10 (2011): 2206–2232, doi:10.1177/016146811111301008.
18. Boggs, *The Next American Revolution,* 72.

ABOUT THE AUTHOR

SOYOUNG PARK IS THE faculty director of online programs in early childhood and childhood special education at the Bank Street Graduate School of Education. A former inclusion and special education teacher, Dr. Park's research and teaching focus on advancing justice for children of color with disabilities, their families, and their teachers. The aim of her community-based scholarship is to transform how educators see and interact with children of color with disabilities and their families, shifting away from deficit-based practices and moving toward humanizing and just approaches. Dr. Park has presented her work nationwide and has published in multiple journals, including *Teachers College Record, Urban Education Journal, Teaching and Teacher Education, Topics in Early Childhood Special Education,* and *Multiple Voices*. She lives in New York with her family.

INDEX